W9-BSU-032

The YANKEE MAGAZINE COOKBOOK

The *YANKEE* MAGAZINE COOKBOOK

by the Editors of *Yankee Magazine*

HARPER & ROW, PUBLISHERS, New York
Cambridge, Philadelphia, San Francisco,
London, Mexico City, São Paulo, Sydney

1817

THE YANKEE MAGAZINE COOKBOOK. Copyright © 1981 by Yankee Magazine. All rights reserved. Printed in the United States of America. No part of this book may be used or reproduced in any manner whatsoever without written permission except in the case of brief quotations embodied in critical articles and reviews. For information address Harper & Row, Publishers, Inc., 10 East 53rd Street, New York, N.Y. 10022. Published simultaneously in Canada by Fitzhenry & Whiteside Limited, Toronto.

FIRST EDITION

Designer: Sheila Lynch

Library of Congress Cataloging in Publication Data

Main entry under title:
The Yankee magazine cookbook.
   Includes index.
   1. Cookery, American—New England.   2. New England—
Social life and customs.   I. Yankee.
TX715.Y18 1981   641.5974   81–47242
ISBN 0–06–014902–7   AACR2

81 82 83 84 85 10 9 8 7 6 5 4 3 2 1

CONTENTS

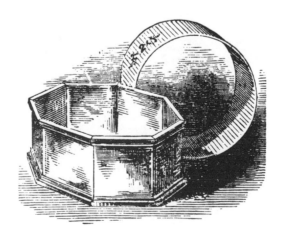

FOREWORD

Mondays are definitely the most fattening days for anyone working at *Yankee* magazine's main office in Dublin, New Hampshire. That's the day the next-door Dublin General Store, with its otherwise daily supply of lunchtime sandwiches, is closed. So that's the day many of *Yankee*'s editors, writers, artists, salespeople, accountants—anyone on the staff who enjoys cooking—arrive at work with covered dishes, huge baskets, towel-draped platters, even pails. In these intriguing containers may be Vermont goat-meat crêpes, lobster quiche, sweet–potato-maple-apple casserole, golden curried potato soup—recently even a whole roasted turkey filled with bourbon-pecan stuffing. Besides being Monday's lunch, this constitutes our official weekly recipe-testing session. Nothing goes into the magazine, and no recipes have gone into this book, without having been subjected to the Monday lunch test.

Food, of course, has always been a part of *Yankee* magazine's existence. In an old diary of *Yankee* founder Robb Sagendorph (1900–1970), I found a November 1935 entry that said, "Long discussion at editorial meeting on the effects of Roosevelt's programs on New England—all over delicious cookies and crackers supplied by Laurie Hillyer." Laurie Hillyer, who has remained associated with us ever since, including as Fiction Editor in the 1970s, continued until her retirement at age eighty-eight to bring all sorts of candies, cookies, sandwiches, and crackers to our weekly editorial conferences. Once in a while, she'd bring some Cross crackers, those exceedingly dry, tasteless, white round crackers known outside New England as Vermont crackers. When I say these were dry I mean exactly that and more. In fact, it was impossible to eat two or three of those crackers with peanut butter without strangling.

To be sure, the very term "Yankee" involves food, at least according to the best definition I've come across. The broadest definition is that most people throughout the world consider a Yankee to be simply an American. To a southerner in the U.S., however, a Yankee is a northerner, to whom it means a New Englander, to whom it means a Vermonter (or a Down Easter or Cape Codder). To many Vermonters, a Yankee is a person who eats apple pie for breakfast. Recently, I asked a Vermont friend of mine who does indeed often eat a piece of apple pie at breakfast time if he felt he was, by the very fact of this morning eating habit, a true Yankee. He doubted it. A true Yankee, he said, would eat his breakfast apple pie "with a knife."

Arguments about the origin of certain Yankee foods and "the only" way to prepare specific traditional dishes have also been an integral part of New England life over the years, and therefore of *Yankee* magazine features. Arguments about Rhode Island jonnycakes, for instance, have included how they originated (Indian vs. settlers), how to spell the word (journey-cake vs. johnny cake vs. jonny cake vs. jonnycake), which kind of corn to grind for jonnycake meal (white flint vs. dent), how to grind that corn (hot and round vs. cool and flat), and, naturally, how to cook them. Not too long ago, this particular argument was formally discussed in the Rhode Island legislature.

Perhaps one of the best-known food controversies is the one involving New England clam chowder and the New York version of clam chowder, which includes, horror of horrors, tomatoes. I recently read in an old cookbook I found in our library (*Monstrous Depravity* by John Gould, published by William Morrow & Co.), the most accommodating explanation of this debate, at least from a New Englander's point of view, that I'd ever come across. "The Maine coast clam is an elongated bivalve and is not the clam of commerce that you find in, say, New York," explains the author. "New York clams are what we call quahogs and no State of Mainer in his right mind eats them. This may explain to you the perennial fuss between New England and New York clam chowder. If a Mainer had to make a clam chowder out of quahogs, he'd put tomatoes in it, too—and garlic and beach plums and chestnuts and about anything else he could think of to improve it."

Sometimes the controversy generated by a *Yankee* article involving a food superlative ("The Best Ice Cream Anywhere," etc.) makes me think we probably should never have put the subject in print. Our article about Charles "Doc" Hall of South Paris, Maine, was an example. For more than a quarter of a century, Doc Hall orchestrated the Oxford Hills Bean-Hole Bean Festival, attended by several hundred local bean-lovers each July. We indicated that Doc Hall's bean-hole beans were the very best to be had in the State of Maine—probably in all of New England. Well, our readers responded by attending his next bean-hole bean festival in such numbers that poor Doc was absolutely inundated with literally thousands of them who, though well-meaning, got in the way and interrupted the delicate cooking procedures to the point that, for the first time in history, Doc's beans came out of the ground burnt to a crisp. (They were still pretty good, I'm told.)

Nonetheless, the price of fame in such cases notwithstanding, our food dialogue with our readers, wherever in the world they may live, has certainly contributed to *Yankee*'s underlying purpose as expressed by Robb Sagendorph in the first issue back in September, 1935. "*Yankee* magazine's destiny," he wrote, "is the expression and perhaps indirectly the preservation of that great culture in which every Yank was born and by which every real Yank must live." I'm comfortable in saying that this book reflects the *Yankee* spirit, and contributes to an understanding of "that great culture."

John Gould has written many things for *Yankee* magazine over the years. He's a Down Easter and knows his New England in all its many facets, including food, from the inside out. Back in the early sixties, he made a statement which, as I reflect upon it now with a few more insights than I had when first coming to Yankee, Inc., twenty-four years ago, is exceedingly profound. "A saucer of real molasses served with biscuits," he said, "is one of the finest experiences of mankind, and corresponds to being elevated to the Supreme Court." I was never absolutely certain whether that was a commentary on New England food or the U.S. Supreme Court. I am certain now, however. At any rate, do plan on reading, enjoying, and using this book for at least twenty-four years, preferably longer. After that length of time, you may be prone to the same sort of dogmatic, opinionated, John Gould–like statement combining food with politics, law, religion, and other weighty matters of the world. Perhaps, too, by then, if you always obey the following Monday-lunch-tested recipes to the letter, you may find yourself eating an occasional piece of apple pie for breakfast. With a knife.

Judson D. Hale, Sr.
EDITOR, *Yankee* magazine and
The Old Farmer's Almanac

POSTSCRIPT: The following, listed alphabetically, are the people who contributed greatly to the creation of this book: Moira Burnham, Mary Cornog, Nancy Crockett, Castle Freeman, Richard Heckman, Veronica Marinaro, Georgia Orcutt, John Pierce, Michael Schuman, Clarissa Silitch, Sharon Smith, *Yankee* magazine Publisher C. R. Trowbridge, and Lila Walz.

Also, participating in the recipe testing were exactly forty people, *Yankee* employees as well as others from the Dublin, New Hampshire, area. Thanks to all.

The YANKEE MAGAZINE COOKBOOK

1

SOUPS, CHOWDERS, AND STEWS

"Soup, Glorious Soup"

Soup ranks with bread as one of the true miracles of civilization. Even before man discovered yeast and gained access to leavened bread, he must have learned the secret of soup. Without either discovery, cooking as an art would never have gotten off the ground.

Soup has the amazing ability to combine bits and pieces of no possible use—except perhaps for fortifying the compost heap or the pig or lying fallow in the refrigerator until moldy—and turning them into delicious, nutritious meals for any number of hungry people. The carcass of a chicken; the picked-over bone of a ham, a scraggly beef bone, a pork bone, a lamb legbone; vegetables left from last night's dinner, and the dinner of three nights ago as well. A few cold potatoes, a cup of cooked rice. Take any of the above, or all, add an onion or two, sliced, a stalk of celery, a bit of salt and pepper, some water, and simmer for a couple of hours—and, from practically nothing, *presto!* comes soup.

Of course, as the following recipes show, you can make excellent soups by starting out with fresh ingredients specifically destined for soup; the results will be at least as good as you get from the random combinations that go into "Left-over Soup." The art of soup has progressed. But never hesitate to resort to the original technique of "anything goes" whenever you need—or want—or the refrigerator dictates good old original soup.

SOUP BASES

Soups fall into two groups: those in which stock is the main liquid; and those in which stock is not. Stocks that form the basis of the first group include beef broth or bouillon, brown stock, white stock (made from chicken, turkey, or veal), consommé, and lamb stock. Stock is also known as broth or (beef or chicken) bouillon.

The second category includes soups based on cream sauce, pureed ingredients in cream, or chunked ingredients in a mixture of cream and stock of some kind. The latter type of soup is known as a "bisque"; although properly speaking a "bisque" should be made of seafood, other soups are today so labeled—tomato bisque, for example.

BEEF BROTH OR BOUILLON

3   pounds lean beef
1   pound marrow bone
6   cups cold water
6   whole peppercorns
1   teaspoon salt
1   medium potato, cut up
1   stalk celery, sliced
1   small onion, sliced
1   small turnip, chopped

Soak meat and bone in water for 1 hour, then bring to boiling. Skim surface, then simmer, covered, for 3 hours. Add seasonings and vegetables, and simmer 2 hours longer. Strain and cool. Skim fat from surface.

Makes 6 cups.

BROWN STOCK

4   tablespoons butter
5   pounds shin beef,
         with bones
2   quarts water
6   whole peppercorns
3   whole cloves
1   bay leaf
1½   teaspoons salt
2   sprigs parsley
1   small potato, sliced
1   small turnip, diced
1   small onion, sliced
1   small carrot, sliced
1   stalk celery, sliced

This broth is slightly stronger in flavor and color than beef broth or bouillon.

Melt butter in large kettle and brown meat. Then soak in water for ½ hour. Bring to boil and skim surface. Cover and simmer 3 hours. Add seasonings and vegetables and simmer 2 hours longer. Strain, cool, and skim fat from surface.

Makes about 3 quarts.

To Clarify Stock

Cool stock thoroughly and remove congealed fat from surface. Measure stock to be clarified, and for each quart use the broken shell and beaten white of 1 egg. Combine stock, shells, and whites, and bring to boil. Boil 5 minutes, then remove from heat. Add ½ cup cold water and cool stock 15 minutes. Strain through cheesecloth. Shell and white will have absorbed impurities and will be caught by the cheesecloth.

WHITE STOCK

This light broth made from chicken, turkey, or veal is the perfect starting point for chicken soups, cream soups, or many light sauces.

Place chicken, carcass, or veal in large kettle and add water. Bring to boiling, and skim surface. Cover and simmer for 3 hours. Add remaining ingredients and simmer 1½ hours longer. Strain twice through double thickness of cheesecloth to achieve a clear stock. Cool and skim.

Makes 2 quarts.

1 broiling chicken, cut up, or chicken or turkey carcass, or 4 pounds veal knuckle
2 quarts cold water
6 whole peppercorns
1 small onion, sliced
2 stalks celery, coarsely chopped
1 bay leaf
1 teaspoon salt

BUTTER BEAN SOUP AND SAUSAGE

A thick soup that can easily take up to a pound of sausage.

In water to cover, soak beans overnight. Drain and combine with 6 cups fresh water in soup pot. Add bay leaf. Bring to boil and simmer, covered, about ½ hour, until beans are tender. Drop potatoes into beans and simmer 15–20 minutes, until potatoes are tender. Melt butter in small saucepan and blend in flour. Dip out 1 cup bean liquid and stir gradually into butter and flour *roux*. Add *roux* to soup and stir thoroughly. Brown sausage well, drain, and add to soup. Add salt and pepper to taste.

Serves 4–6.

1 pound dry lima or broad beans
6 cups water
1 bay leaf
4 medium potatoes, peeled and diced
4 tablespoons butter
2 tablespoons flour
½ pound sausage, bulk or removed from casings
Salt and pepper

2 cups black beans
1 quart water
1 ham bone
4 quarts ham broth or
     water
1 pound stewing beef,
     cut small
1 medium onion,
     chopped
1 medium carrot,
     scraped
     and grated
2 stalks celery, diced
   Salt and pepper
2 tablespoons butter
2 tablespoons flour
⅓ cup sherry
2 to 3 hard-boiled eggs,
     quartered
2 to 3 lemons,
     quartered

BLACK BEAN SOUP

An elegant soup high in protein, a favorite for Sunday lunch in New England.

Soak beans in 1 quart water overnight. Drain. Put into large kettle with ham bone, ham broth or water, beef, onion, carrot, and celery. Bring to boil and simmer, covered, until beans are soft—about 3–4 hours. Dip out and discard meat and ham bone. Puree soup in blender or sieve. Season to taste with salt and pepper. Rub butter and flour together and form into 2 small balls. Place in soup. Return soup to kettle and bring to boil. Turn down heat and stir until thickened. Add sherry. Pour soup into individual soup bowls. Serve with each bowl 1 lemon quarter and 1 hard-boiled egg quarter.

Serves 8–10.

Necessity Soup

And then there's always the time when you've been snowed in for three days straight, and haven't been to the store for four days before that, and the cupboard is absolutely bare. How to feed a family? Brew up some Necessity Soup, that's how.

Look again. The hens are laying at least one or two eggs a day. There are a couple of bouillon cubes left in the cupboard, or perhaps a can of broth. Some crusts of bread, a bit of butter. A can of beans, or a package of frozen peas from last summer's garden? Already more than enough ingredients for this kind of soup. If even a cup of milk is around, you're home free. Toast the bread until really crisp, then fry it in a little butter if you have any. Combine bouillon cubes or broth with four cups of water— or more, if you have more cubes—and throw in an onion, sliced, if there *is* an onion, and maybe a diced potato or two. Add vegetable(s), if any. Simmer all this for half an hour. Beat the eggs lightly in a bowl, then gradually stir into the soup. Add the cup of milk, if you have it, and float bread on top. Superb. Use as many or as few of these ingredients, or others you might have on hand, as you like. It's astonishing what will make soup.

JELLIED CLAM BROTH

A lovely way to start a summer luncheon.

Soften the gelatin in cold water and then add the hot broth and stir until dissolved. Add chilled grapefruit juice, salt, and lemon juice. Stir to blend, then pour into 4 to 8 (1 cup into 4 or ½ cup into 8) individual bowls and chill.

Serves 4–8.

2	tablespoons unflavored gelatin
1	cup cold water
2	cups hot clam broth
1	cup grapefruit juice, chilled
⅛	teaspoon salt
½	teaspoon lemon juice

COCK-A-LEEKIE

Leeks lend a subtle flavor to this traditional Scottish chicken soup.

Combine chicken, seasonings, parsley, and water in large pot and simmer for 2 hours. Take out chicken, take meat from bones, and chop. Set aside. Cool broth, then skim off fat. Add to broth rice, leeks, and chopped chicken meat. Simmer 45 minutes, until rice and leeks are tender.

Serves 6–8.

1	chicken or other fowl
1	whole clove
	Dash mace
6	peppercorns
	Salt and pepper
1	sprig parsley
2	quarts water
¼	cup uncooked rice
6	leeks, washed and chopped

CRAB AND TOMATO BISQUE

2 tablespoons butter
2 tablespoons flour
2 cups rich milk
½ teaspoon salt
⅛ teaspoon pepper
1 cup flaked crab meat
1 cup tomato juice
2 tablespoons finely
    minced parsley

Serve this creamy pink treat in patty shells for a lovely luncheon.

In saucepan, melt butter, add flour, and blend. Add milk gradually and cook till thickened, stirring constantly. Add seasonings and crab meat and simmer for a few minutes. Just before serving, heat tomato juice in another pan. When hot, add tomato juice gradually to first mixture and serve immediately, sprinkling parsley over each serving.

Serves 4.

COLD CUCUMBER SOUP

1 tablespoon olive oil
1 medium onion, sliced
3 medium cucumbers, diced
1 teaspoon cornstarch
3 cups chicken broth
1 teaspoon salt
    Pepper to taste
½ teaspoon dried basil
¼ cup dry vermouth or
    dry white wine
1 cup sour cream for garnish

Made like any hot soup, then chilled. Smooth and cool on a hot day.

Heat oil in bottom of kettle and sauté onion until wilted. Add cucumbers. Combine cornstarch with a little of the broth and add to kettle. Stir in remaining broth, salt, pepper, and basil. Stir mixture and bring to boil. Cover and simmer 30 minutes. Puree in sieve or blender. Stir in vermouth or other wine, and chill thoroughly—2 hours or longer. Garnish with sour cream.

Serves 4–6.

LENTIL SOUP

2 cups dried lentils
1 quart water
4 slices bacon, diced
2 medium onions, chopped
2 medium carrots, chopped
3 quarts water
1 cup celery, diced
2 teaspoons salt
1 teaspoon pepper
½ teaspoon dried thyme
2 bay leaves
3 medium potatoes, peeled
1 ham bone, or 3 slices
    bacon, diced
2 tablespoons vinegar

A wonderfully hearty, whole-meal soup.

Wash lentils. Sauté bacon until crisp. Remove from pan and set aside. Sauté onions and carrots in bacon fat until golden. Combine lentils, 3 quarts water, celery, salt, pepper, thyme, bacon, onions, carrots, and bay leaves in 4-quart kettle. Grate potatoes and add to soup along with ham bone or bacon. Cover kettle and simmer soup 1 hour, until lentils are tender. Remove bay leaves. Lift out ham bone and cut off meat; put meat back into soup. At serving time, stir in vinegar.

Makes about 3 quarts soup.

Aging and Freezing Soups

Soups, like stews, have the enviable ability to improve with age—not *old* age, but a soup made the day before it is to be used, refrigerated overnight, and reheated, will have had time for the component parts to blend their flavors to produce a mellow whole.

Soup can be kept two or three days in the refrigerator, or frozen for longer storage; it freezes beautifully. To use frozen soup, simply place in double boiler over boiling water and allow to thaw. Then heat as desired.

HEARTY FISH SOUP

Toast thick slices of French bread and float them in the soup at serving time.

In large kettle, heat oil and sauté onion, parsley, and garlic in it. Drain clams and add enough water to juice to measure 1 quart. Add liquid to kettle. Add tomatoes or tomato sauce, salt, thyme, bay leaf, and pepper, and simmer 30 minutes. Cut fish into good-sized pieces and add to soup. Cover and simmer 10 minutes. Add shrimp and clams and simmer 5 minutes more. Ladle soup into bowls and float bread rounds on top.

Serves 8–10.

2 **tablespoons olive oil**
1 **medium onion, sliced**
¼ **cup minced fresh parsley**
1 **clove garlic, minced**
10 **ounces shelled, cooked clams, with juice**
Water
1 **quart stewed tomatoes or tomato sauce**
1 **teaspoon salt**
½ **teaspoon thyme**
1 **bay leaf**
Pepper
1½ **pounds fish—halibut, haddock, or sole**
1 **pound shelled, de-veined raw shrimp**
1 **loaf French bread, sliced diagonally ½-inch thick**

CREAM OF MUSHROOM SOUP

1 pound fresh mushrooms
4 tablespoons butter
1 medium onion, chopped
2 tablespoons flour
6 cups milk, or 4 cups milk
   and 2 cups cream
1 bay leaf
4 sprigs parsley
1 whole clove
   Dash mace
   Salt and pepper
   Dash cayenne
½ cup heavy cream
2 beaten egg yolks

Incomparably better than the canned version. Serve garnished with cheese croutons.

Clean mushrooms, chop coarsely, and put through blender or chopper. Melt butter in double boiler top. Add onion and mushrooms and cook for 5 minutes over direct heat, stirring frequently. Sprinkle flour into mixture and blend thoroughly. Gradually stir in milk or milk and cream, stirring continuously. Add seasonings, and stir until mixture thickens slightly and boils. Place pot over hot water and simmer covered for 20 minutes, stirring frequently. Combine heavy cream and egg yolks and stir a little hot soup into them. Then stir them into bulk of hot soup.

Serves 6–8.

KATY'S SPECIAL ONION SOUP

7 large onions
¼ pound butter
½ cup flour
1 gallon brown stock or
   beef broth, heated
1 bunch parsley
2 bay leaves
2 cloves of garlic
   Salt and pepper
¼ cup Worcestershire sauce
   Croutons
   Grated Parmesan cheese

A traditional French onion soup topped with croutons and melted cheese.

Cut onions into quarters, then cut in thin cross-section slices. Sauté in butter until golden brown. Add flour and blend well. Then add hot stock and let simmer for 20 minutes. Tie up in cheesecloth parsley, bay leaves, and garlic, and add to soup. Boil for a few minutes and then remove cheesecloth bag. Season to taste with salt and pepper, and add Worcestershire sauce. Pour into individual soup cups. Top with croutons and grated cheese. Melt cheese under broiler for a few minutes just before serving.

Makes 1 gallon.

OXTAIL SOUP

2 pounds oxtails
   Flour
3 tablespoons butter
   Water or beef broth
   to cover
1 bay leaf
1 cup diced carrots
1 cup chopped onions
1 cup diced potatoes
1 cup diced celery
   Salt and pepper

Rich brown broth laced with vegetables.

Chop oxtails into short sections. Sprinkle with flour. Melt butter in kettle and brown sections. Add water or broth to cover and add bay leaf. Cover, bring to boil, turn down heat, and simmer 1 hour. Strain broth, reserve meat, and add vegetables to strained broth. Simmer 15–20 minutes, until vegetables are tender. Cut meat from bones, dice, and add to soup. Bring soup to boil, season to taste with salt and pepper, and serve.

Serves 10.

UNCLE HARRY'S PEA SOUP

Easy to make, and a superb first course.

Cook peas and onion in beef bouillon (undiluted). Puree peas and onion with bouillon in blender or sieve. Sauté mushrooms in butter until tender. Stir mushrooms and ½ cup of the whipped cream into puree, and season to taste with salt and pepper. Heat gently until the soup is hot. Stir in sherry. Ladle into individual bowls, and top each bowl with generous spoonful of whipped cream.

Serves 4.

1 package (10 ounces) frozen peas
1 onion, minced
1 can beef bouillon
4 to 5 medium mushrooms, sliced
2 tablespoons butter
1 cup whipped cream
Salt and pepper to taste
1 tablespoon sherry

PUMPKIN OR SQUASH SOUP

A frequent item on colonial menus, still good.

Combine milk, onions, and bay leaf and scald. Strain milk and combine with chicken broth and mashed pumpkin or squash. In separate pan, melt butter and stir in flour. Gradually add in milk mixture, stirring after each addition until mixture is smooth. Add salt and pepper, and cook, stirring constantly, for 5 minutes, until soup is hot and almost boils.

Serves 6–8.

2 cups milk
2 sliced onions
Small piece bay leaf
2 cups chicken broth
2 cups cooked, mashed pumpkin or winter squash
3 tablespoons butter
3 tablespoons flour
1 teaspoon salt
Dash white pepper

OYSTER BISQUE

Creamy-smooth oyster-flavored soup for very special occasions.

Chop oysters. Add water, celery, leek, onion, parsley, clove, bay leaf, and rice. Bring slowly to boil and simmer, covered, 45 minutes. Press through sieve and add remaining seasonings, milk, and optional peas. Stir in combined egg yolk and cream, bring to boil, and serve.

Serves 6–8.

1 pint oysters
2 cups water
1 stalk celery
1 leek, halved
1 slice onion
1 sprig parsley
1 whole clove
½ bay leaf
¼ cup uncooked rice
1 teaspoon salt
¾ teaspoon paprika
¼ teaspoon pepper
¼ teaspoon cayenne
Dash nutmeg
1 cup scalded milk
½ cup cooked peas (optional)
1 egg yolk, beaten
1 cup cream

FRESH STRAWBERRY SOUP

1 quart fresh strawberries,
 or 2 packages (10 ounces
 each) frozen
 unsweetened berries
2 cups warm water
4 tablespoons sugar
2 tablespoons cornstarch
 or quick tapioca
 Dash salt
 Dash cinnamon
2 tablespoons lime or
 lemon juice
⅛ teaspoon vanilla
1 cup sour cream

Good hot or cold. For variety, substitute raspberries or blueberries. Serve like other soups—as the first course—or, as the Scandinavians do, for dessert!

Wash and hull strawberries. Combine with water and puree in blender or sieve. In saucepan, combine sugar, cornstarch or tapioca, salt, and cinnamon. Stir in puree and bring mixture to boiling point. Simmer gently just until soup becomes slightly thick and clear. Stir in lime juice and vanilla. Spoon into bowls and top with sour cream. Or chill thoroughly and then serve topped with sour cream.

Serves 4–6.

CREAM OF WATERCRESS SOUP

1 cup chopped watercress
2 cups chicken broth
4 tablespoons butter
4 tablespoons flour
¼ teaspoon salt
 Dash white pepper
2 cups milk
1 tablespoon chopped
 fresh chives

Tangy made with watercress, this is also good made with spinach or lettuce instead. Add a speck of nutmeg to spinach soup instead of chives.

Combine watercress and broth and simmer 5 minutes. In separate pan, melt butter and stir in flour. Gradually add broth and watercress, stirring well after each addition to make mixture smooth. Add salt and pepper. Stir in milk and heat just to boiling point. Serve garnished with chopped chives.

Serves 4.

A *"Recipe with a History"*

by Minnie C. Bradley

As children, we lived with our parents in the back woods of Plaistow, New Hampshire, the only Town of that name in the whole United States of America. Every Sunday in summer, Father hitched the horse to our two-seater Democrat buggy and Mother took us five kids on a treasure hunt for red raspberries, black raspberries or running vine blackberries; sometimes we found a blueberry bush. We were poking along when Mother espied a specially large patch of red raspberries. We filled our little tin lard pails in no time and all got back into the buggy, intending to go back home, but then Mother saw a very large turtle cross the road just beyond us.

She scrambled out of the buggy and gave chase. By a quick maneuver, she flipped the monster onto his back and yelled to me to fetch "that short piece of rope under the seat!" We managed to capture the critter's hind leg, tying it stoutly with the rope; the other end of the rope she wound around the rear axle and knotted securely. There the huge reptile hung suspended until we reached home.

"Good gorry! Woman, what have you been doing now?" my father exclaimed. That turtle weighed 26 pounds! The meat tasted like chicken and was white like chicken breast.

MOTHER'S TURTLE SOUP

8	pounds turtle meat, cut into chunks
3	tablespoons salt
	Water to cover
1	large onion, cut fine
2	stalks celery, cut fine
½	teaspoon white pepper
	Dumplings (p. 12)

Simmer turtle in salted water very slowly for about 2 hours in large kettle. Add onion, celery, and pepper, and simmer another ½ hour. Liquid should be reduced by half by now. Add flour dumplings, cover kettle, and cook 12 minutes more. A gourmet's dish, if one can catch the turtle!

GARNISHES FOR SOUP

There are lots of ways to dress up soup to make it look even more inviting—fillips that add eye appeal, texture contrast, or taste. Here are some suggestions.

CROUTONS

4 slices thinly sliced
   bread, a few days old
1 egg, beaten
4 tablespoons grated cheese
2 tablespoons butter

Can be simply toasted, buttered crumbs, or as below. These croutons stay crisp longer in soup. For ultimate crispness, pass in separate bowl and let diners help themselves. Good with almost any soup, chowder, or stew.

Cut crusts from bread. Toast slices on one side under broiler. Combine egg with cheese and beat in butter. Coat untoasted side of bread slices with mixture. Toast in 350°F. oven until golden. Cut into fine cubes.

Makes plenty to serve 4–6.

DUMPLINGS

4 tablespoons butter
½ cup boiling water
¾ cup flour
¼ teaspoon salt
   Dash paprika
3 eggs
¼ cup grated cheddar cheese

Use in the lighter soups with a stock base. Soup must be boiling to properly cook dumplings. The soup can contain vegetables, but should not have potatoes as an ingredient, nor salt pork or other fatty meat.

Melt butter in water and cook for 2 minutes. Stir in flour, salt, and paprika, and cook, stirring, until mixture becomes quite thick. Cool slightly. Beat in eggs one at a time. Beat in cheese. Drop by spoonfuls into boiling soup, or fry in deep fat, drain, and serve in soup.

Makes about 24.

Spinach Dumplings

1 cup cooked, drained
   spinach
1 cup fine dry bread
   crumbs
1 egg white, beaten
   lightly

Chop spinach and stir in crumbs and egg white. Let stand 10 minutes. Shape into small balls and drop into boiling soup. Cook 5 minutes.

Makes about 18.

The Farm Kitchen

by Margaret Carmichael

When the lumbering grey snow clouds have snuffed out the last flickers of light from the worn-out winter sun, when a bristling North-Easter begins to flap the old shingles on the barn roof and swoop about up among the rafters, when the cattle stamp and chew and swish their tails as if to keep warm, there is no place on earth that looks quite so good to a man as his own old-fashioned farm kitchen. The dog, too, knows what that final shutting of the barn door means, and rising from his bed in the hay, follows his master's lantern between the snow drifts to the shed door, where the cat whines on the cold granite step. There is food, warmth, and a corner for each one of them within the four sturdy walls of the farmer's kitchen. Let the city-folk have their big living-rooms and parlors with their noisy radiators tucked away in corners. What radiator ever baked a crock of beans on a Saturday night, simmered a pot of soup all day, or had an oven door that a man could let down to warm his feet on? In the farm kitchen, where the big black range is, there, also, is the very essence of *home*.

—Excerpt from March 1936 *Yankee*

OTHER GARNISHES

Crispy fried salt pork scraps (use with chowders)
Bits of crisp bacon (chowders or cream soups)
Julienne strips of ham (cream soups or consommé)
Grated cheese (thick soups and, of course, onion soup)
Sliced fried sausage (thick soups)
Buttered popcorn (cream soups)
Sliced toasted almonds (cream soups)
Salted whipped cream (vegetable soups)
Thin avocado slices dipped in lemon juice
Sour cream (beet soups)
Capers
Lemon slices or wedges (clear soups)
Chopped ripe olives, green olives, or stuffed olives
    (clear or cream soups)
Chopped fresh herbs, especially dill, parsley, or chives
Sliced or grated hard-boiled eggs (bean soups)

Chowders and Stews

SOUP or CHOWDER or STEW??

They look like soup, they taste like soup, but in New England, chowders and stews are *not* soup!

A New Englander knows the difference between a soup and a chowder or a chowder and a stew almost instinctively, but then New Englanders have had plenty of time to digest and perfect these distinctions. Indeed, among those brought up to know the differences, there is a tacit understanding that the qualities of each species need never be mentioned.

But not everyone is so blessed, and for those not privy by birthright to the distinctions between chowders, stews, and soups, here they are:

Chowders, no matter what the eponymous ingredient may be—clams, corn, vegetables, whatever—*always* contain milk and potatoes. And usually onion, salt pork or bacon bits, and broth.

Stews, as in oyster stew, are identical to chowders except that they do *not* contain potatoes, and often harbor more solid matter in proportion to liquid than is usual in chowders.

Soups, on the other hand, may contain an enormous variety of ingredients, may call themselves after any one of the many items they contain, but never use milk as the decisive feature of their soupiness. Cream soups contain sauce thickened with flour; some other soups contain cream itself; still others are thickened by grated potato or pureed vegetable. So-called Manhattan clam chowder, that anathema of chowder lovers, is really clam soup (by which name it is only slightly less offensive to a true New Englander).

Where "Chowder" Came From

Chaudière in French means a big cooking pot or cauldron. The word came to Newfoundland from France with the fishermen who settled there. Gradually the term came to refer to the contents of the cauldron: *faire la chaudière* ("to prepare the pot") was done by each fisherman putting something in the community pot. New Englanders soon turned the word to "chowder."

CLAM CHOWDER

True New England–style chowder, with just clams, onion, potatoes, and salt pork. Serve with "common" crackers, which are plain, unsalted crackers, or with soda crackers.

Dice salt pork and cook until crisp in saucepan; remove pork scraps and set aside. Sauté onion in pork fat or butter until golden. Add potatoes and just enough water to be seen. Season with salt and pepper, then cover, bring to boil, turn down, and simmer until potatoes are just tender. Add clams, bring to simmer again, and cook for just 2 minutes longer. Add hot milk. Season to taste and serve, adding pork scraps or butter dots if desired.

Serves 4.

⅛ pound salt pork, or
    2 tablespoons butter
1 onion, diced or chopped
2 good-sized potatoes,
    peeled and sliced
    or diced
    Salt and pepper to taste
1 pint minced fresh sea
    clams
1 quart rich milk, scalded

CORN CHOWDER

An old-time recipe that is still fantastic—some just aren't!

Fry bacon until crisp. Drain and reserve. Sauté onions in fat until tender, then transfer to 2-quart pot along with potatoes, corn, bouillon cube, and water. Cover and cook 15 minutes. Add milk and heat almost to boiling. Add salt and pepper to taste, ladle into bowls, and garnish with crumbled bacon.

Serves 4–6.

4 slices bacon
3 medium onions, sliced
4 medium potatoes, sliced
1 package (10 ounces)
    frozen corn, or
    1½ cups fresh corn
1 bouillon cube
1 cup water
3 cups milk
    Salt and pepper

Fishermen's Rules

When the wind is in the East,
Then the fishes bite the least.
When the wind is in the West,
Then the fishes bite the best.
When the wind is in the North
Then the fishes do come forth.
When the wind is in the South
It blows the bait into the fishes' mouth.

FISH CHOWDER

To make when the winds are favorable!

2 ounces salt pork, diced, or 3 tablespoons butter
1 small onion, minced
2 cups raw, peeled, diced potatoes
Hot water
Salt and pepper
1½ pounds haddock fillets
½ teaspoon thyme
2 cups hot milk
½ cup warm light cream
1½ tablespoons butter, cut up

In Dutch oven, fry out salt pork until fat is rendered. Remove pork scraps. Or melt butter. In fat or butter, sauté onion until golden. Add potatoes, hot water to cover, and salt and pepper. Place fish on top. Cover and simmer until potatoes are done and fish flakes. Add thyme, milk, and cream. Stir well and heat through (do not boil). Dot with butter and serve. (If you used salt pork, sprinkle with crisp pork scraps.)

Serves 4–6.

VEGETABLE CHOWDER

A good, hefty chowder.

1 cup carrots, sliced
½ cup green peas
⅓ cup celery, chopped
½ cup cabbage, chopped
1 medium onion, sliced
1 medium potato, peeled and diced
Boiling water
1 bouillon cube
¼ teaspoon pepper
2 tablespoons butter
2½ cups milk
1 cup cream

Cook vegetables in boiling water to barely cover for 15 minutes, or until tender. Add bouillon cube and pepper. Stir in butter and milk, and bring almost to boil. Stir in cream and heat through. Serve immediately.

Serves 6.

Lobster Stew

Like the issue of boiled versus steamed lobster (p. 49), the question of lobster stew is fraught with controversy. In the July 1972 *Yankee,* author Margaret Koehler called it "the best left-over dish in the world." This is certainly accurate, but it is also true that where a little lobster must go a long way, the meat from a single boiled (or steamed!) lobster cooked expressly for a lobster stew will serve four, rather than one. Like oyster "stew," lobster stew is more soup than stew, but similarly, it can be served like a soup, as a first course with chowder crackers, or, with salad and rolls, as a perfectly adequate supper.

Some recipes require the stew to be simmered only a few minutes; others insist that the stew should be aged—for from two or three minutes on the back of the stove, to five or six *hours* in the refrigerator—and then reheated. Clam broth is used with cream in some, milk and cream in others, and sometimes only milk is called for (but remember, the "rich milk" called for in old recipes had a hefty cream content).

Basic Proportions of Lobster Stew to Serve Four Persons

Use the larger amount of lobster meat and butter for a main-dish stew; the smaller for a "soup stew."

1 **to 3 cups cooked, diced lobster meat**
3 **to 5 tablespoons melted butter**
1 **quart scalded liquid (2 cups cream and 2 cups milk; 3½ cups light cream and ½ cup clam broth; 3 cups evaporated milk and 1 cup water; or 4 cups evaporated milk)**
Salt and pepper

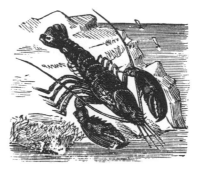

HEARTY LOBSTER STEW

¼ cup butter
2 cups boiled lobster meat,
      cut in pieces
1 quart scalded milk or
      half-and-half
   Salt and pepper

A good stew to serve as a main course. The "aging" in the refrigerator brings out the true and delicate flavor of the lobster.

Melt butter in heavy kettle over low heat. Add lobster and cook slowly until the rich pink of the lobster colors the butter, stirring constantly to prevent burning. Remove from heat, cool slightly, and slowly stir in scalded milk or half-and-half. Add salt and pepper to taste. Refrigerate stew for 5–6 hours. Reheat before serving.

Serves 2–4.

MAINE LOBSTER STEW

1 cup cooked lobster meat
3 tablespoons melted
      butter
3½ cups warmed light cream
½ cup warm clam broth
      or juice
   Pinch salt
   Pinch paprika
   Few grains cayenne

One up for the clam broth faction. Once you've tasted lobster stew made this way, you'll find that the fishy-vinegary tang lent by the broth renders the all-milk stew bland by comparison. But—a matter of taste!

Sauté lobster meat in butter for 3 minutes, until sizzling. Stir in cream and clam broth or juice. Add seasonings. Let sit away from heat for 2 minutes to "marry" flavors. Then reheat to boiling point and serve.

Serves 2–4.

Maine.

OYSTER STEW

¼ cup butter
1 quart oysters
1 quart warmed milk
      (or half milk
      and half cream)
1½ teaspoons salt
   Pepper
1 teaspoon paprika

Made without flour, the colonial way.

Melt butter, add oysters, and cook 1 minute, or until edges curl. Add milk, salt, pepper, and paprika, bring almost to boiling point, and serve at once with oyster crackers.

Serves 4.

GRANDMOTHER'S PARSNIP STEW

This tastes best made a day ahead and reheated. Use parsnips that have been frozen in the ground all winter if possible; they are far better.

Sauté bacon until crisp. Remove and drain bacon. Set aside and keep in warm place. Pour off all but 2 tablespoons fat. Sauté chopped onion in fat until golden. Add potatoes and parsnips and brown lightly. Pour water into pot and add half the bacon and the parsley. Simmer until vegetables are tender, about 20 minutes. Pour milk over crackers and let soak briefly, then add to vegetables along with salt and pepper. Reheat. Dot with butter and remaining bacon.

Serves 6–8.

6 **slices bacon, diced**
1 **medium onion, chopped**
2 **cups raw, peeled, cubed potatoes**
2 **cups raw, coarsely chopped parsnips**
3 **cups boiling water**
½ **cup snipped parsley**
4 **cups scalded milk**
1 **cup crushed oyster crackers**
  Salt and pepper
2 **tablespoons butter, cut up**

MEATS, GAME, AND POULTRY

Meats

BEEF AND VEAL

The rib roast, once a standard Sunday dinner, is now a rarity, both because of its cost and because families are smaller. Most other cuts of beef remain as popular as ever.

Veal, alas, is not just high priced, but often astronomical, *if* you can find it. This, too, reflects change in our way of life. When more people lived in the country, on small farms, there was always a veal calf or two, but it's sure hard to raise one in a city apartment, which is where more people live today!

BEEF AND OYSTERS IN WINE

2 pounds round steak
Worcestershire sauce
1 clove garlic, halved
2 tablespoons butter
1 pint oysters, with liquor
1 tablespoon cornstarch
¼ cup red wine, preferably port

Steak topped with oyster-and-wine sauce.

Brush steak with Worcestershire sauce and rub with halves of garlic clove. Melt butter in skillet and brown steaks on both sides, cooking about 5 minutes on each side, or to desired degree of doneness. Place on platter and keep warm. Drain liquor from oysters and combine liquid with cornstarch. Briefly cook oysters in pan drippings, just until edges curl. Place on platter with steak and keep warm. Add oyster liquor and cornstarch to skillet. Add wine. Cook over low heat, stirring, until mixture thickens and becomes clear. Return steak and oysters to pan and heat through.

Serves 4.

Roast Beef and Strawberry Shortcake

by O. L. Persechini

"Church Supper Tonight"—in large red letters, the words pop into view on the white canvas banner that has just been raised on the lawn of the Congregational Church in Rindge, New Hampshire, one of only two or three meeting houses in the state that have served both church and town since colonial days.

It's time for supper, and the hungry guests, who have been waiting quietly in the vestry, stream into the hall. There is good-natured jostling as friends and family find seats together. Finally, the 112 places of the first sitting have been settled into, strangers introduce themselves, and the fragrant platters, bowls, and baskets heaped with roast beef, candied carrots, mashed potatoes, green salad, and homemade bread are passed around the tables. Waiters move in to gather tickets, pour the first of gallons of piping-hot coffee, and replenish the serving dishes as fast as they are emptied and handed up. After second and third helpings for those who want them, there will be freshly-baked strawberry shortcake with whipped cream. There will be no let-up until the tables have been cleared and reset for the second sitting and the hall and kitchen again are in apple-pie order.

—Excerpt from article originally titled
"May I Have a Slice of Rare, Please?" in October 1974 *Yankee*

BEEF CARBONNADE

Stew flavored with onions and beer.

4   to 6 medium onions
2   pounds stewing beef, cut
        in chunks
3   tablespoons flour
4   tablespoons oil
2   cups dark beer
¼   teaspoon allspice
1   bay leaf
⅛   teaspoon thyme
        Salt to taste
¼   teaspoon pepper

Slice onions. Dredge beef chunks in flour and brown in oil in Dutch oven. Add onions and cook until tender. Pour in beer and add spices, stirring to blend. Cover and cook 1½ hours, until meat is very tender.

Serves 4–6.

SWISS STEAK BURGUNDY

Steak smothered in wine and vegetables.

3   tablespoons flour
½   teaspoon pepper
2   pounds round steak,
        1 to 2 inches thick
2   tablespoons butter
1½ cups tomatoes, fresh or
        canned, drained
½   cup minced shallots
6   medium mushrooms,
        chopped
2   stalks celery, sliced thin
1   large or 2 medium
        carrots, sliced thin
1   clove garlic, minced
1   teaspoon salt
½   cup Burgundy wine

Combine flour and pepper and coat steak with mixture. In large skillet or Dutch oven, melt butter, and brown meat well on both sides. Combine tomatoes, shallots, mushrooms, celery, carrots, garlic, salt, and wine and pour over meat. Cover tightly and simmer for 2 hours, until meat is very tender. Lift meat out onto serving platter and spoon sauce over it.

Serves 4–6.

VEAL WITH ALMONDS

Substitute boned chicken breasts for veal for greater economy. Serve with mashed potatoes and cranberry sauce.

3   to 4 pounds boneless veal
3   tablespoons flour
1   to 1½ teaspoons salt
1   teaspoon paprika
1   cup blanched,
        chopped almonds
1   to 2 cups stock
        (use beef cube)
¼   pound mushrooms,
        coarsely chopped
        (or 4½-ounce can,
        drained)
3   to 4 tablespoons butter
1   cup cream

Cut veal in 1- to 2-inch cubes. Dredge with flour seasoned with salt and paprika. Combine almonds with stock and simmer for about 30 minutes. Sauté mushrooms 4 or 5 minutes in 1 tablespoon of the butter. Remove to Dutch oven. Add remaining butter to skillet and brown meat. Place browned meat in Dutch oven. Rinse out frying pan with almond stock and pour over meat. Simmer, covered, for 1 hour, or until meat is very tender. Add cream and simmer another 5 minutes. Taste sauce for further seasoning.

Serves 8.

LAMB

Right up to the 1960s, lamb was everyday fare, but from then on, reasonable lamb, like reasonable veal, became increasingly a casualty of the population shift. People in their twenties today often spurn what is now a delicacy simply because they've never had it. And indeed, except in certain ethnic communities where lamb is still in demand, lamb is rarely offered in the supermarkets where most of us shop. Nevertheless, if you are not now a lamb fan, the following recipes will make you one!

CHARLOTTE'S SWEDISH LAMB

Perhaps the best roast lamb you've ever tasted. The odd combination of ingredients really works.

Combine salt and pepper and rub into lamb. Place lamb in roasting pan, fat side down. Cover top with onions and carrots. In bowl, combine coffee, sugar, cream, and boiling water. Pour into bottom of pan. Bake at 350°F. for 2½ hours. Then scrape onions and carrots off top of lamb, and turn roast over so fat side is up. Return to oven and roast ½ hour longer. Lift lamb to serving platter and keep warm. Make gravy from juices remaining in pan.

Serves 6–8.

1	tablespoon salt
1	teaspoon pepper
1	7- or 8-pound leg of lamb
2	cups grated onion
2	cups grated carrots
4	tablespoons instant coffee
4	tablespoons sugar
½	cup light cream
4	cups boiling water

CHIVE-BAKED LAMB ROAST

Long, slow cooking bakes flavors right in and gives extra tenderness.

Place lamb on rack in roasting pan. Bake at 300°F. for 2 hours. Pour off fat. Combine chives, lemon juice, mustard, and rosemary; mix well. Pour over lamb. Sprinkle with pepper. Bake 1–2 hours more, or until meat thermometer registers 170–180°F. (depending upon desired degree of doneness).

Serves 6.

1	5-pound leg of lamb
¼	cup chopped fresh chives
½	cup lemon juice
2	tablespoons prepared mustard
¾	teaspoon rosemary Pepper

A Note from A Hog Reeve

by L. K. Little

"Cornish, N.H., Mar. 10, 1971. From Our Own Correspondent: At the annual Cornish Town Meeting last night, L. K. Little, retired Inspector General of the Chinese Customs Service, was unanimously elected Hog Reeve."

I wasn't there to receive the honor (being in the Virgin Islands at the time). But as soon as I discovered that I had been chosen as hog reeve, I took steps to find out something about the definition of the term and the responsibilities of the position. These steps took me to my bookcase and the Oxford Dictionary. Of course, I knew that a hog was a grown-up pig, but what was a reeve? (To tell the truth, I didn't know whether the word was a noun or a verb.)

Imagine my pride when I read in definition (1) that a reeve was "an old English official of high rank, having a local jurisdiction under the king." I should have stopped right there, because definition (2) stated that a reeve is a "local official of minor rank; an overseer of a parish; a churchwarden or the like."

It is now time to confess that I was only one of six hog reeves elected at Town Meeting. My fellow reeves would, I am sure, agree with me that the office is far from demanding. We never held a meeting, nor were we ever called on to reeve a hog. In fact, during my years in Cornish I have never seen a hog; and my guess is that there are more reeves than hogs in town.

I notice in the Town Report that next above the Hog Reeve in the hierarchy of town officers is the Surveyor of Bark and Timber; above him comes the Fence Viewer. These are all honorable offices dating back some 200 years. Who knows but that I may one day be chosen for one of these other positions? I realize that, at 82, my political prospects are somewhat uncertain; but my motto is *nil desperandum,* and I am prepared to go the whole hog to serve my beautiful town.

—Excerpt from article originally titled
"A Hog Reeve," in March 1975 *Yankee*

PORK

The pig is a boon to mankind from New England to Djakarta and points West or East, depending on the standpoint, and has been for centuries. Almost every land has it that roast pork was discovered after a tremendous fire *somewhere*, be it forest, prairie, grasslands, or town, depending on the locale of the legend, when the odor of the burned pig was so enticing that survivors of the fire took a bite. And indeed the taste of pork roasted, stewed, fried, chopped, ground, salted, smoked, or curried, remains the stuff of legend.

Pork was the basis of inland New England economy long before beef; the family pig sustained many a household over the long hard winter, providing bacon, salt pork, hams, sausage, and lard, not to mention soap!

CROWN ROAST OF PORK

A royal dish. Serve for holidays instead of turkey. Allow about one rib per person.

1 10- to 12-rib crown roast of pork
3 to 4 potatoes, cut up, or aluminum foil
4 to 6 slices bacon
Salt, pepper, flour
1 head cauliflower, steamed

Cover tips of roast bones with pieces of potato or foil to prevent burning. Wrap bacon around base of roast. Rub meat with salt, pepper, and flour. Fill center with Cranberry Stuffing or Savory Stuffing (see below) and roast at 350°F. for 40 minutes per pound. When done, remove potato or foil and garnish ribs with paper frills. Place cauliflower head, intact, in center and serve.

Serves 10–12.

Savory Stuffing

Combine all ingredients and work with hands to blend thoroughly. Pile in center of roast.

3 cups cracker or dry bread crumbs
1 cup ground lamb or veal
1 cup ground beef
2 medium apples, peeled, cored, and chopped
3 tablespoons minced onion
1 teaspoon salt
½ teaspoon pepper
1 teaspoon sage
1 teaspoon thyme
1 tablespoon dried parsley
¼ cup melted butter

Cranberry Stuffing

1½   cups cranberries
¼   cup water
4   tablespoons sugar
½   cup melted butter
4   cups bread crumbs
1   teaspoon salt
     Dash pepper
¼   teaspoon thyme
⅛   teaspoon dill weed
1   tablespoon grated onion
1   clove garlic, crushed

Cook cranberries in water until berries pop, about 10 minutes. Combine with remaining ingredients and pile in center of crown roast.

YANKEE PORK TENDERLOIN

Flour-coated tenderloin cooked in sour cream.

1   pork tenderloin,
       1½ pounds
½   cup flour
2   to 3 tablespoons butter
1   onion, chopped
1   teaspoon salt
½   teaspoon pepper
¾   cup sour cream

Cut tenderloin into thick slices and roll in flour. Place in frying pan with butter and onion, sprinkle with salt and pepper, and brown on both sides. Baste with sour cream and cook, covered, over low heat for about 30 minutes or until tender.

Serves 4–6.

PORK SHOULDER ROAST WITH SPICY SAUCE

This roast is subtly flavored all the way through.

1   fresh picnic shoulder
       of pork (5 to 6 pounds)
     Salt and pepper
2   small onions, minced
1   tablespoon
       Worcestershire sauce
1   tablespoon sugar
½   teaspoon paprika
¼   cup vinegar
½   cup water
2   tablespoons catsup

Have picnic shoulder boned and rolled at market. Season with salt and pepper. Place on rack in roasting pan. Combine remaining ingredients and spoon over roast. Bake at 350°F. until pork is cooked through, about 30 minutes per pound. Baste frequently with pan juices during baking. Skim fat from juices and serve them as sauce.

Serves 6–8.

NEVER-FORGET PORK CHOPS

Chops with a tangy tingle.

2   cloves garlic
1   teaspoon salt
12   pork chops, 1 inch thick
1   cup vinegar
1   cup water
3   tablespoons pickling
       spice

Crush garlic cloves and combine with salt in the bottom of a glass or enamel roasting pan. Add the chops, vinegar, water, and spice. Allow to stand, refrigerated, for at least 10 hours, turning occasionally. Drain and bake at 325°F. for 60 minutes.

Serves 8–10.

HEAD CHEESE

How to use every bit of the pig, from "tail to grunt."

Cut head into four pieces. Remove eyes, brain, and ears, and clean out snout. Place head pieces and tail in large kettle and cover with boiling water. Add 1 tablespoon salt. Boil until flesh begins to fall from bones, about 1½ hours. Skim surface often during boiling. Lift meat from kettle and allow to cool slightly. Pick all meat from bones, and remove as much fat as possible. Grind meat coarsely and season to taste with salt, pepper, and sage. Skim fat from cooled broth, and add enough broth to ground mixture to soften it. Pack into greased loaf pans or molds. Refrigerate or freeze. To serve, slice and fry.

Makes about 1½ pounds head cheese.

1 **pig's head**
1 **pig's tail**
   Boiling water
   Salt
   Pepper
   Ground sage

HAM

Today, and our forebears would think it odd, every ham you buy at the supermarket is completely cooked. In fact uncooked ham or ham slices are hard to find and very expensive if you can find them (always discounting the possibility of a friendly neighbor with pigs who smokes his own!). Recipes for marinating ham before baking are obsolete, as the label on a modern supermarket ham states quite unabashedly, "water added and gelatin filled." Once a poor old ham has been injected with all that, no wonder it can't—and won't—absorb marinade. A "processed" ham, or one that has been already simmered, but without water or gelatin added, can be marinated to some extent before cooking. Should you happen to come across that rarity—a smoked, un-processed, un-everything ham—here's what to do with it.

Scrub well, trim off hard black pieces, put in large kettle, and cover with cold water. Bring water to boil, lower heat, and *simmer* ham for 30 minutes per pound. ("Boiled" ham is *never* boiled!) A boiled ham is done when the skin peels off easily. Remove from heat and allow to cool in water. Remove from kettle and peel off skin. Bake at 350°F. for 2 hours, then take from oven, cut off all but about 1 inch of fat, and score that in a diamond pattern. Insert whole cloves at intersections of score lines. Make a glaze out of 1 teaspoon flour, 1 cup brown sugar, 1 teaspoon dry mustard, and 2 tablespoons vinegar and brush over top of ham. Return to oven, basting frequently, for 20 minutes.

OLD NORTH SHORE SMOTHERED HAM

Ham slice, 1½ to 2 inches thick
¼ teaspoon ground cloves
Warm water
1½ cups stale bread crumbs
1½ cups scalded milk
½ teaspoon salt
½ teaspoon ground cinnamon
1 small onion, chopped and diced fine
¾ to 1 cup brown sugar

The ham is moist and fork tender, and the topping is browned and pleasantly crisp. The combination of flavors (from the top down: brown sugar, cinnamon, onion, milk-soaked bread crumbs, and ground cloves) is unexpectedly stupendous. Serves 6–8 persons generously with a single slice of ham.

If ham slice is from an uncooked ham, cover with cold water and simmer for 45 minutes on top of stove. Drain. Place cooked ham slice in greased baking pan or greased 12-inch iron skillet. Sprinkle with ground cloves. Pour warm water into skillet around ham until water comes halfway up the ham slice. Mix bread crumbs with milk, salt, cinnamon, and onion. Pile on top of ham slice to even thickness. Cover with brown sugar—enough to form a ½-inch crust over bread crumb layer. Bake at 350°F. for 50–60 minutes. Cut in wedges like a pie and serve.

Serves 6–8.

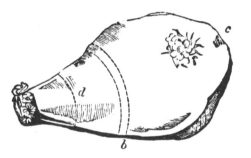

CRANBERRY HAM STEAK SANDWICH

2 slices ham, ¾ to 1 inch thick, each
2 tablespoons whole cloves
3 cups cranberries
1½ cups honey

An old-time New Englander. Serve with a good hot mustard.

Slash fat surrounding ham every 2 or 3 inches to prevent curling during cooking. Stud fat with cloves. Mix cranberries and honey. Place 1 slice ham in buttered baking dish to fit and cover with half the cranberry mixture. Top with second slice and cover with remaining cranberry mixture. Bake at 350°F. for about 1½ hours, or until done, basting occasionally.

Serves 6–8.

Game

A funny thing, game. . . . Rock Cornish *game* hens are *not* game, and may not be *hens*, either, whereas wood*cock*, which may be *hens*, *are* game. Moose, which are game, and look like it, behave and taste more like cattle! Rabbit is—and isn't—game, depending on whether you bag a wild one in the woods, or buy a domestic rabbit raised for eating. The wild ones do have a gamey flavor, and are much leaner and tougher—always marinate wild rabbit before cooking. A well-fed domestic rabbit doesn't need marination, does taste like chicken, and has dark and light meat—like woodcock, too, except that with woodcock it is the breast that is dark, and the legs that are light. One sure thing, though, venison is *always* game! Hang and age, as beef, before cutting up and freezing or cooking.

Did You Know. . . ?

Deer hardly ever move more than twenty miles from where they were born. Most live within a five mile radius. They are what conservationists term an "edge" animal, choosing a habitat of mixed woods and fields. They are not plentiful in areas of extensive forest; in fact the major cause of the amazing increase of deer in the last 100 years is the cutting down of the coniferous forests, resulting in mixed hardwoods of varying age compositions.

—Excerpt from November 1953 *Yankee*

VENISON STEW

3 pounds cubed venison
2 tablespoons flour
2 tablespoons butter
   Salt and pepper
   Hot water
6 medium potatoes,
      quartered
6 medium carrots, sliced
4 small turnips, quartered
1 package (10 ounces)
      frozen peas
1 can (10 ounces) tomatoes,
      drained
2 tablespoons flour
1 can (12 ounces) beer
1 cup white wine

Hunter's stew with a ''venis-geance''!

Dredge meat pieces in 2 tablespoons flour, then brown in butter in skillet. Place in deep 4-quart casserole and season with salt and pepper. Add hot water almost to cover and simmer 1½ hours. Add remaining ingredients and simmer 30 minutes longer, until vegetables and meat are tender. Serve with hot baking powder biscuits (p. 118) or fresh bread.

Serves 6–8.

RABBIT WITH MUSTARD SAUCE

1 rabbit, wild or domestic
2 tablespoons lemon juice
4 cups (about) water
½ cup flour
   Pepper
2 tablespoons butter
1 medium onion, minced
1 clove garlic, crushed
6 medium mushrooms,
      sliced
3 tablespoons flour
1 teaspoon tomato paste
1½ cups rabbit or chicken
      stock
½ cup white wine
½ cup sour cream
2 tablespoons dry mustard
½ teaspoon dried tarragon,
      or 2 sprigs fresh
      tarragon, chopped

Rabbit may be bought frozen or from a supplier who raises rabbit for meat. Either way, this dish is absolutely superb. Good with chicken, too.

Cut rabbit into serving pieces. If using wild rabbit, soak in mixture of lemon juice and water for 2 hours. Drain, dry, and dust with ½ cup flour and pepper. Melt butter in skillet and brown rabbit pieces in it. Remove pieces with slotted spoon and reserve. Sauté onion and garlic in pan. Add mushrooms and cook until tender. Stir in 3 tablespoons flour and tomato paste and continue stirring until smooth. Gradually stir in stock and wine, and continue stirring until mixture boils. Combine sour cream and mustard and stir into gravy. Lay rabbit pieces in gravy and sprinkle with tarragon. Cover and cook over low heat about 1 hour, until rabbit is tender. Place rabbit on serving plate, spoon gravy over it, and serve with rice.

Serves 6.

About Woodcock and How to Cook It

Not one person in a hundred has ever seen one!

by John Stuart Martin

Reasons for the obscurity of *Philohela minor*, "the little swamp-lover" (or bog-sucker, night partridge, hookum pake, Labrador twister, mud snipe, timberdoodle, big eyes), are several. While not the all-night bird that owls and whippoorwills are, the woodcock's most active hours are the two or three just before and just after dawn and dusk.

Actually a shore bird that has moved inland, the woodcock neither perches off the ground nor struts by day in the open. It walks, feeds, and rests on bosky, mucky turf or in high-ground thickets too dense for easy walking. When you do step near one, unless the light is fading, it will more likely sit tight than take wing. From ten feet you can look straight at one that is squatting amid dead leaves, and unless you catch its eyeshine you will not make out its form.

When it does spring up, the start of its flight is so erratic, so full of cuts, curvets, dipseys, and doodles, that the unwonted eye is baffled and the bird's definition lost. Only a blurred impression remains, of a bird about the flicker's size but chestier, chunkier, and with wider, crookeder wings, a much longer bill, darkish back, bright buff front and belly, and a short, tucked-in tail that is white-tipped underneath. You will also notice that, like a mourning dove, its wings whicker or whistle. Unlike any other bird it is quite likely to circle sharply and pitch right back at your feet whence it sprang. In this event you will find yourself looking into the weirdest little face you ever saw, with a bill like a brown plastic syringe and big, black bug-eyes as close together as a grasshopper's on top of its ball-shaped head.

All this would be interesting enough in a songbird, but the woodcock is preeminently a game bird; that is, sporty to hunt, tasty to eat.

ROAST WOODCOCK

If there were no other cause for our enthusiasm, what comes out of the oven after you put some woodcock in would amply suffice. Again perversely, the deep breast is dark meat instead of white, which is what the plump legs and thighs are. You roast the little critters in foil wrapped loosely but with the edges crimped shut, for 25–30 minutes at 250°F. Then flare the foil open and brown the breast at 400°F. until the bacon strips, which you have pinned on with wooden toothpicks, crisp and blacken. In serving, under-lay each bird with a thick slice of pale toast to sop up the fat-rich gravy. Though the plumpest female will not oven-dress seven ounces, or a male more than five, I defy the average eater to get down more than two whole woodcock at a sitting, their flesh is that rich.

—Excerpt from article originally titled
"Little Swamp Lover," in October 1970 *Yankee*

POULTRY

President Herbert Hoover's promise of "a chicken in every pot," once considered rash, has certainly been fulfilled. One of the most versatile of all meats, chicken is also one of the least expensive. A real blessing, as there are at least a million marvelous chicken dishes, many of which for taste can more than hold their own at the most luxurious banquet, dripping with champagne, oysters, and caviar!

Aside from being the center of attraction at Thanksgiving and Christmas dinner, turkey can be used to advantage in most all recipes calling for cooked chicken.

Duck and goose are both dark meated and richer than chicken or turkey, with the heavy allotment of fat common to waterfowl, but *if cooked properly*, they are superb—tender, crisp skinned, and free from fat. As a side benefit, you get fine, tasteless fat you can use as shortening—or to rub on a child's sore throat!

CHICKEN BREASTS IN CREAM

Lightly flavored and very *elegant.*

Rub breasts with lemon juice, place in 9-x-13-inch baking pan, and sprinkle with salt, white pepper, and thyme, then brush with melted butter. Bake at 350°F. for about 45 minutes, until chicken is just tender. Take from oven, remove chicken breasts to platter, and keep warm. Into juices from baking pan stir broth and vermouth. Bring to boil over high heat and cook until volume is reduced by half. Stir in cream and simmer until slightly thickened. Add lemon juice. Pour sauce over warm chicken breasts, sprinkle with minced parsley, and serve over rice.

Serves 4–6.

4 whole chicken breasts, halved, boned, and skinned
½ teaspoon lemon juice
Salt and white pepper
1 teaspoon thyme
4 tablespoons melted butter
¼ cup chicken broth
¼ cup dry white vermouth
1 cup heavy cream
1 tablespoon lemon juice
Minced parsley

CHRISTMAS CHICKEN

Baked under a Yorkshire pudding roof, this is a good dish for a small Christmas. Don't open the oven door while pudding is baking!

Combine flour with salt and pepper and roll chicken pieces in it. Melt butter in skillet and brown chicken. Place browned chicken in greased 9-x-13-inch baking pan, skin side up, and bake at 350°F. for 20 minutes. Meanwhile, make Yorkshire Pudding (see below). Take chicken from oven and pour pudding batter over and around chicken in baking pan. Bake at 350°F. for 40–50 minutes longer, until batter is puffed and golden, and chicken is tender. Serve with Mushroom Sauce (see p. 66).

Serves 4–6.

½ cup flour
Salt and pepper
2 tablespoons butter
1 broiling chicken, cut up

Yorkshire Pudding

Beat flour, salt, milk and water into eggs, continuing to beat until large bubbles rise. Pour over chicken in pan as described above.

1 cup flour
½ teaspoon salt
½ cup milk
½ cup water
2 eggs, beaten

ROCK CORNISH GAME HENS IN CURRANT SAUCE

2 medium carrots
3 stalks celery
10 ounces mushrooms, fresh
   or canned, drained
4 shallots
1 small onion
6 game hens
   Spicy prepared mustard
2 tablespoons flour
2 cups chicken broth
½ teaspoon ground oregano
¼ teaspoon pepper
1 tablespoon currant jelly

Game hens are produced by cross-breeding Plymouth Rock chickens and Cornish Game fowl.

Dice carrots, celery, mushrooms, shallots, and onion very finely and spread in bottom of shallow roasting pan big enough to hold game hens. Rub hens with mustard and place on diced mixture. Place pan in oven heated to 450°F., and brown hens evenly on all sides, turning often. Reduce heat to 350°F. and roast hens breast up until tender—40–50 minutes. Remove game hens from pan. Into contents of pan stir flour. Slowly stir in broth and cook over low heat to thicken. Stir in oregano, pepper, and currant jelly and simmer gently 15 minutes to reduce sauce. Then return game hens to pan, spoon sauce over them, and return to oven for 10 minutes. Place game hens on serving platter, spoon sauce into sauce boat, and serve.

Serves 6.

The First "Jingle Bells"

by Frank W. Lovering

When sleighing parties were the acme of winter fun, "Jingle Bells" echoed, winter after winter, through the crisp air on starlit nights. But the story of this song's birth begins on a bright November morning in 1850 when a young man named James Pierpont leaves his father's brick home in West Medford, Massachusetts, with music on his lips and the words and score of a lyric in his pocket. He is gaily humming a tune as he walks the mile or so to the home of a friend.

He knocks at the door of Mrs. Mary Gleason Waterman's house and, when invited in, tells her, "Mary, I've written a little song, and I'd like to try it out on your piano." He sits down and runs through a lively melody.

"That's a merry jingle! I like it!" Mary exclaims.

On the instant, "Jingle Bells" is born—and for some 112 years now, the tune has been lilting merrily around the world.

It has been sung nearly everywhere, even in Russia. Elizabeth Green, a graduate of Jackson College in Medford, visited Russia with a delegation of American youth and tells of hearing, in a home for the children of railroad workers, this song sung by a chorus of one hundred youngsters from eight to sixteen years old. The words were in Russian, but the tune and the emphasis were wholly James Pierpont's!

—Excerpt from December 1962 *Yankee*

OVEN-FRIED HERB-MUSTARD CHICKEN BREASTS

Crisply baked with a delicious basting sauce.

Wash chicken breasts, dry, and place in a 9-x-9-inch baking pan. Brush with some of the oil and bake at 425°F. for 30–40 minutes, or until browned. Reduce temperature to 300°F., brush again with oil, and bake 15 minutes longer. Combine remaining oil with mustard, vinegar, garlic, onion, herbs, and pepper, and spoon over chicken. Bake 20–30 minutes longer, basting pieces with juices from pan, until pieces are tender.

Serves 4.

2	whole chicken breasts, halved
½	cup olive oil, or other cooking oil
2	tablespoons prepared mustard
2	tablespoons vinegar
1	clove garlic, minced
2	tablespoons grated onion
2	tablespoons minced fresh parsley, or 2 teaspoons dried
½	teaspoon savory
	Dash white pepper

1   small roasting chicken
2   tablespoons softened
       butter
3   cups cooked rice
¼   cup minced cooked ham
1   sautéed, chopped
       chicken liver
2   tablespoons blanched
       almonds
1   tablespoon minced
       fresh parsley
2   tablespoons melted butter
½   teaspoon salt
¼   teaspoon pepper
¼   cup sherry

SHERRIED ROAST CHICKEN

Sherry on the outside, stuffing on the inside make this chicken special.

Rub chicken all over with softened butter. Combine remaining ingredients except sherry to make stuffing. Fill chicken's cavities loosely. Place chicken in roasting pan and bake at 350°F. for 1½ hours, basting with sherry every 15 minutes, until chicken is done. Spoon pan juices over chicken when served.

Serves 4.

1   10-pound turkey
½   cup (about 2 strips)
       bacon, cut up
12 tiny onions
5   cups dry bread crumbs
¼   teaspoon ground cloves
       Turkey liver, gizzard,
       and heart, sautéed
       and chopped
4   celery tops, chopped
       Salt and pepper
¼   teaspoon celery seed
1   teaspoon summer savory
1   teaspoon sage
1   teaspoon Worcestershire
       sauce
1½ cups turkey broth
¼   cup grape juice or red
       wine
½   cup boiling water
       Butter

ROAST TURKEY WITH GIBLET STUFFING

Basic, beautiful baking method for a holiday feast.

Clean turkey and rinse cavities. Sauté bacon in skillet until crisp. Add onions to skillet and sauté until lightly colored. Spoon contents of skillet over bread crumbs in large bowl. Stir in remaining ingredients except butter and boiling water, blending to distribute moisture evenly. Fill turkey cavities loosely with stuffing, sew or skewer closed, and rub turkey with butter. Place turkey on rack breast down in roasting pan and place pan in oven preheated to 400°F. Roast 25 minutes. Pour boiling water into pan, reduce oven heat to 350°F., and bake for about 2½ hours longer, until thigh meat is tender when pinched and leg joint moves easily when leg is wiggled. Turn bird breast up for last ½ hour of baking time to brown top. Remove turkey to platter and let stand 10 minutes before carving.

Serves 8–10.

Talking Turkey in Bennington

by Rob Woolmington

When the Bennington Chapter of the National Wild Turkey Federation holds its spring dinner and calling contest, Vermont English competes all night with yelps and gobbles. The only turkey-talking competition in New England, the evening's program draws men and women who cackle and cluck just like the hens and toms that are successfully repopulating the hillsides of Vermont.

After dinner the calling starts. John Randolph of Bennington, former editor of *The Vermont Sportsman* and a widely published outdoors writer, explains the rules to contestants as the judges gather behind a screen. Randolph will request each of the four required calls—similar to technical exercises in ice skating—and then the talker can slide his tongue freestyle in the "caller's favorite." Randolph gives the word: "the yelp." The hall is silent as the contestant strains his face and then lets out a piercing yelp. You expect wild turkeys to march through the front door, so clearly does his yelp resound.

Each talker next must "cluck" and then imitate the "kee kee run." The latter is a sound produced by poults in autumn; an excitable, rhythmic chant, it goads the talkers to pout and grimace in fitting preparation for the gobble.

The gobble, of course, is the pinnacle of achievement in turkey talking. One man gobbles by shaking his head and blithering an extended vowel. Yet another takes a small rubber hose with latex within and shakes it hard, harder, dancing up and down like a medicine man. Yet another stands quietly for some seconds. The audience moves restlessly—then he nearly doubles over with a fierce gobble. It is so quick, and he has bent so far forward, that you can't see how he did it. But then the judges never see.

The caller's favorite is nearly always the cackle; these reverberate and seem to laugh, but after a gobble they are pure anticlimax.

Thirty-eight callers, the youngest age seven, come and perform. Then the judges huddle and the audience become animated.

The judges return with their verdicts. A tie is registered in the junior division. A seven-year-old from Rutland must compete with a girl, probably 13, from Bennington. They yelp and cluck, kee kee and cackle. Another break. The judges ask for sudden-death call-off, of the talker's choice. All is still. Seven-year-old Carl Wedin gobbles, splendidly. There are murmurs. His opponent gives a fine call too. Pause. The judges huddle. Carl Wedin receives their nod.

With great gusto, the audience gobbles and clucks its appreciation.

—Excerpt from May 1980 *Yankee*

A Revolutionary Thanksgiving
(St. Johnsbury, Vermont, A.D. 1776)

The following account is taken from a letter from Juliana Smith of St. Johnsbury to her cousin, Mrs. Betsey Robinson of Newton, Massachusetts; it sounds remarkably contemporary!

"All the baking of pies and cakes was done at our house and we had the big oven heated and filled twice each day for three days before it was all done, and everything was *good,* though we did have to do without some things that ought to be used.

"Neither Love nor Money could buy Raisins, but our good red cherries, dried without the pits, did almost as well, and happily Uncle Simeon still had some spices in store.

"We had a fine red Deer so that we had a good haunch of Venison on each table. These were balanced by huge Chines of Roast Pork at the other ends of the Tables. Then there was on one a big Roast Turkey and on the other a Goose and two big Pigeon Pasties.

"Then there was an abundance of good Vegetables of all the old Sorts and one which I do not believe you have yet seen. Uncle Simeon had imported the Seede from England just before the War began and only this Year was there enough for Table use.

"It is called Sellery and you eat it without cooking. It is very good served with meats.

"Our Mince Pies were good although we had to use dried Cherries as I told you, and the meat was shoulder of Venison. The Pumpkin Pies, Apple Tarts, and big Indian Puddings lacked for nothing save Appetite by the time we had got round to them.

"There was no Plumb Pudding, but a boiled Suet Pudding, stirred thick with dried Plumbs and Cherries, was called by the old Name and answered the purpose. All the other spice had been used in the Mince Pies, so for this Pudding we used a jar of West India Preserved Ginger which chanced to be left of the last shipment which Uncle Simeon had from there.

"We did not rise from the table until it was quite dark, and then when the dishes had been cleared away, we all got round the fire as close as we could and cracked nuts and sang songs and told stories."

—Excerpt from article originally titled
"Thanksgiving, 1776: a Day of Fasting and Prayer," by Louise C. Marston,
and submitted by Marjorie Elliott, in the November 1972 *Yankee*

ROAST GOOSE

Serve with Lemon Apples or Glazed Pears (see p. 145 and p. 146) as a side dish. Red cabbage is the traditional vegetable.

**1 young goose
(10 to 12 pounds)
Melted butter**

Have goose cleaned and drawn, and trim appendages. Wash thoroughly inside and out and drain. Cover with cold water and soak 15 minutes. Drain and pat dry. Place on rack in roasting pan. Prick skin all over. Place in oven preheated to 450°F. for 20 minutes. Siphon or spoon fat from pan as it accumulates. Turn oven down to 325°F., and roast for 3½–4 hours. The last hour or so, baste goose with melted butter.

Serves 6.

SPICED ROAST DUCK

Crisply baked, subtly seasoned. The apple acts to absorb fat from the inside and should be discarded when the duck is taken from the oven.

**1 teaspoon curry powder
1 clove garlic, minced
¼ teaspoon Tabasco
1 teaspoon turmeric
1 duckling
1 small apple, peeled
¼ cup honey
¼ cup each lemon and
    orange juice
1 teaspoon curry powder**

Combine first 4 ingredients and rub inside of duck with mixture. Place apple in cavity. Prick skin of duck all over. Place on rack in roasting pan. Put in 450°F. oven for 20 minutes; drain off fat. Turn oven down to 325°F. and bake for 2 hours, basting occasionally with mixture of honey, juices, and curry.

Serves 4.

3

SEAFOOD AND FISH

Seafood

Like corn, the fruits of the sea were the very foundation of New England; without them, the early colonists would undoubtedly have starved. Puritan Governor Bradford of Massachusetts, who once complained that "our poor people have nothing but lobster to eat," would be surprised to learn that no longer can one pick up enormous lobsters at low tide in Boston harbor, nor decry the annual glut of salmon choking the majestic Connecticut River, but he would surely delight in the recipes that follow as gleefully as the twentieth-century trencherman. (Indeed, from all accounts, he would probably eat at least twice as much!)

Nevertheless, though rarer and dearer today than in Bradford's time, fish and seafood still constitute the basis of the economy in many New England towns and still figure largely in the New England diet. Thanks to our long and convoluted seacoast and many beaches, seafood is still very much a way of life to the coastal Yankee, however transplanted.

Buying Guide for Seafood and Fish

The quantities given below are for amounts of meat or "unadorned" dishes, not stews, scallops, or casseroles.

BUY	FOR
2 pounds King crab legs	3 cups crab meat
1 can (6½ ounces) crab meat	To serve 2 persons
A 2-pound lobster (the ratio is roughly 2 to 1, live lobster to cooked meat, for average-sized lobsters. For lobsters over 6 pounds, you will get more meat per pound)	1 pound lobster meat
1 quart unshucked clams to serve as "steamers"	To serve 1 person as a main course
8–12 unshucked clams to serve as "steamers"	To serve 1 person as an appetizer
6 oysters on the half shell	To serve 1 person as a main course
2 oysters on the half shell	To serve 1 person as an appetizer
1 pound bay scallops	To serve 4 persons
1 pound shrimp in the shell	To serve 3 persons
½ pound shelled shrimp	To serve 3 persons
1 can (4½ ounces) shrimp	To serve 2 persons
1 pound fish fillets, fresh or frozen	To serve 4 persons
2–4 smelts	To serve 1 person
1 brook trout	To serve 1 person
1 lake trout	To serve 2 persons
½ pound fresh salmon	To serve 2 persons
1 can (1 pound) salmon	To serve 4 persons
A 5-pound striped bass	To serve 8 persons
1 pound salt cod	To serve 3–4 persons
Fresh cod or other large fresh fish	Allow ½ pound per person for whole fish
½ pound scrod (or young codfish)	As above
½ pound salt mackerel	To serve 1 person
1 large salt herring	To serve 2 persons
A 3-pound shad	To serve 6 persons
1 pair shad roe	To serve 2 persons
A 4-pound bluefish	To serve 6–8 persons

CLAMS

Joe Allen, the one and only *Yankee* "Oracle," said once, "the cussed clam is so tied up with the original colonizing of New England that it is a job at times to separate the clams from the colonists." He claimed that the fabled taciturnity of old Yankees was based on their acquaintance with the clam— "A clam don't say nuthin'." Clammed up, in fact.

STEAMED CLAMS

Fresh (live)
 unshucked clams
Water
Clam broth
Melted butter
Lemon juice or vinegar
Pepper
Butter lumps

Plan on about a quart of unshucked clams per person. No special "steamer" vessel is needed; any kettle with a tight cover will do. A canning kettle is fine. For a complete meal, serve with a tossed green salad and bread, and with a cup of hot clam broth or "liquor." Or, if you have managed only a small number of clams, serve two or three clams per person, with a smaller helping of broth, if desired, as an appetizer. Dip the clams in melted butter, sip the broth, and enjoy!

Wash clams in several waters to remove as much sand as possible, and scrub shells. Put into kettle and add water until you can *just* see the water level. Some cooks use boiling water, others use cold—it doesn't much matter. Boiling water may save a minute or so, but the clams will lower its temperature almost immediately to warm. Try it both ways, and use what works best for you. Cover kettle tightly and bring to boil. When the water boils, turn heat down to low and let simmer, steaming clams for 10–15 minutes, or until shells open. Drain off, strain, and reserve liquid. This is the clam broth, or liquor. Serve clams in a separate bowl for each person with individual dishes of melted butter to which a few drops of lemon juice or vinegar are added. Alongside each helping of steamers, serve a cup of hot clam broth sprinkled with pepper and topped with a lump of butter.

HENRY MELIX'S WAMPANOAG CLAM PIE

An authentic and delicious Indian treat that serves 10 generously, made in a deep-dish pie plate (the same recipe, halved, makes a regular nine-inch pie). Drain off the liquor the clams come in and rinse them well before grinding. After they are ground, there will be plenty of liquor. Drain off that liquor, reserving half a cup for the "clam juice" specified below.

1   cup lard
3   cups flour
½   teaspoon salt
½   to ¾ cup cold water

Pastry

Cut lard into flour mixed with salt. Add water and mix well until pastry "cleans the bowl." Form into ball and refrigerate while you make filling. Then roll out to make bottom and top crusts.

Filling

Mix clams, eggs, onion, crumbs, and liquid. Try out salt pork until browned. Dip out browned pork scraps and reserve. Add 4 tablespoons salt pork drippings to clam mixture, along with salt and pepper. Line a 10-inch deep-dish pie plate with pastry and sprinkle half the pork scraps over it. Put in clam mixture and top with remaining pork scraps. Cover pie with pastry, seal edges, and bake at 425°F. for 15 minutes. Then lower oven heat to 325°F. and bake for 40 minutes longer.

Serves 10.

1   quart ground clams
2   eggs, beaten
3   tablespoons grated onion
1   cup fine cracker crumbs
½   cup clam juice (or water or milk)
½   pound salt pork, diced
     Black pepper and salt to taste

A Rhode Island Barrel Clambake

by Horace G. Belcher

It has been said that the chief contribution of the Indians to the New England pioneers was the clambake. A family bake, or one for a small group, may easily be made in a barrel. The best barrel bake I know of is that of Capt. Herbert M. Knowles, long Superintendent of the Third Life Saving District before the U.S. Life Saving Service was incorporated in the Coast Guard. Here is Capt. Knowles' bake:

"Make cheesecloth bags for clams, sweet and Irish potatoes, corn, and everything except lobsters, chicken, and fish provided you include these. The bag for clams should be broad enough to allow the clams to spread out over the barrel. The fish should be split in half and placed on shingles wrapped in cheesecloth, so each piece may be handled by unwrapping the cloth and sliding onto a platter. Lobsters may be thrown in the bake in any way.

"Stones about the size of two bowls put together are about the right size. Wood should be packed up crossways, with shavings, etc., underneath, with the stones packed in with the wood up toward the top of the barrel before lighting. Then add wood until the stones get hot. They turn white when of the proper heat. Set the barrel as deeply into sand as you wish. You cannot get it too deep. Put about three inches of sand or gravel in the bottom of the barrel and place pieces of scrap sheet iron around the sides of the barrel. These scraps can be had at any tin shop without cost. The sand and scrap iron prevent the stones from burning bottom and sides of barrel. The stones are picked up with a six-tine fork, when hot, and packed around well. If hot enough they will break and stow good.

"Be sure to have everything for the bake ready to go in the barrel as soon as the stones are put in. The green corn husks should be soaked in salt water and added with the first layer of rockweed over the stones. Then lay in the clam bag, spreading it out as much as possible. Pack your lobsters around this, then lay in the potatoes, fish, chicken, and such other things as you may add.

"Spread a wet or moist bag over the bake and fill the barrel up tightly with wet seaweed. If you have a wash tub handy, turn it over the top of the barrel and apply wet seaweed around it to hold in the steam.

"Hold your ear to the side of the barrel and when you hear the ingredients of the bake growling, which should be within a few minutes after steam starts making, you will know that all is well. The bake should be ready to open in about 45 minutes to an hour from that time. I never saw one cooked too long and I once had one in about three hours. To my surprise it turned out to be one of the best bakes I ever had.

"Saving the corn husks and soaking them to lay over the stones with the seaweed, gives the bake a sweetness which cannot be obtained in any other way."

—Excerpt from article originally titled
"A Rhode Island Clambake," in May 1939 *Yankee*

CLAM-BAKE SAUCE

Melt the butter in a saucepan and stir in the vinegar and lemon juice. Add seasonings and continue stirring. When well mixed, cover and let simmer.

Makes about 1 quart.

1	pound butter
1	pint tarragon vinegar
1	teaspoon Tabasco sauce
	Juice of one lemon
1	tablespoon salt
2½	ounces Worcestershire sauce

OYSTERS

A veritable mine of iodine, copper, manganese, and vitamins A, B, C, and D, oysters also contain about three times as much iron as spinach. Health is the oyster's real pearl. Like clams, oysters don't say much ("close as an oyster"), but their taste is eloquent. Buy them shucked, for unless you have an expert in the house, it will take a couple of hours to pry them loose from their shells. For recipes requiring serving oysters on the half-shell, you must either have a competent fish-monger close by, or become an expert at shucking oysters yourself! Always warm milk before adding it to oysters or oyster liquor; otherwise, the milk will curdle.

CURRIED OYSTERS

A creamy oyster casserole with just a hint of curry. Allow a good two hours to drain the oysters in a colander.

Melt butter and sauté oysters over low heat until they plump out, and the edges curl slightly. Combine flour with salt, pepper, and curry powder and sprinkle over oysters. Then sprinkle lemon juice over all. Remove oysters from heat. Beat mayonnaise, cream, mustard, and chives together until well blended. Fold in oysters. Turn into a 2-quart casserole and top with buttered bread cubes. Bake in 400°F. oven for 15 minutes.

Serves 6.

¼	cup butter
1	quart shucked oysters, drained
3	tablespoons flour
½	teaspoon salt
¼	teaspoon pepper
¼	teaspoon curry powder
2	tablespoons lemon juice
½	cup mayonnaise
1	cup cream (or evaporated milk)
2	tablespoons prepared mustard
1	tablespoon minced chives
1½	cups buttered bread cubes

SCALLOPED OYSTERS

1 cup cracker crumbs
⅓ cup melted butter
1 pint oysters, drained
  and picked over
  (reserve liquor)
  Salt and pepper
½ cup warm cream or
  half-and-half
  Oyster liquor, strained

Scallop was the old-time term for mixtures baked in milk or in a cream sauce and served in a scallop shell. The term scallop has since been extended to a number of dishes baked in milk or in a cream sauce, but not served in a scallop shell—scalloped potatoes, for example. This recipe is simple, old-fashioned, and very good.

Butter shallow 6-x-10-inch baking dish, and sprinkle a layer of cracker crumbs on bottom. Pour a little melted butter over crumbs. Add a layer of oysters, and sprinkle with salt and pepper and more melted butter. Repeat. Do not have more than 2 oyster layers. Mix cream or half-and-half with oyster liquor and pour over dish. Top with remaining crumbs and melted butter and bake at 400°F. for 30 minutes.

Serves 6.

ELEGANT OYSTERS

½ cup butter
½ cup flour
1 cup milk
1½ teaspoons paprika
½ teaspoon salt
¼ teaspoon black pepper
  Dash cayenne
1 onion, finely chopped
½ green pepper,
  finely chopped
½ clove garlic, minced
1 teaspoon lemon juice
1 tablespoon
  Worcestershire
  sauce
1 quart oysters
  (picked over and heated
  in the liquor)
½ cup crushed soda or
  common crackers

Rich and luxurious "company" dish. Serve with rice and fresh peas, asparagus, or braised endive.

Melt butter, blend in flour, and cook gently until lightly browned, stirring. Add milk and cook until sauce thickens. Add paprika, salt, pepper, and cayenne, and blend. Then add onion, green pepper, and garlic. Cook slowly for 5 minutes. Remove from heat and add lemon juice and Worcestershire sauce. Mix in oysters and pour into greased 2-quart baking dish. Sprinkle cracker crumbs over top and bake at 400°F. for 30 minutes.

Serves 8.

SCALLOPS

These delicate, white-fleshed shellfish possess one of the handsomest, and certainly one of the most symmetrical, shells in the sea. The very word "shell" brings to many minds unfamiliar with the sea the image of a scallop shell, symbol of the international Shell Oil Company. The recipes below are for shelled scallops, but, should you be lucky enough to obtain the shells, scrub them well and keep to bake and serve scalloped or deviled seafood in (or anything else). Scallop shells are the traditional receptacles in which to serve the French *coquilles*, best known of which is perhaps the *Coquilles St. Jacques*, made with crab meat. "Bay" scallops are two-and-one-half to three-and-one-half inches in diameter; "Cape" scallops are much smaller—one to two inches.

Sautéed Scallops

Cut large scallops in half. Dredge in flour and sauté in melted butter for 2–3 minutes on each side.

Broiled Scallops

Dot scallops with butter and broil 3–4 minutes. Turn, dot with butter, sprinkle with fine cracker crumbs, and broil about 2–3 minutes more.

LOBSTERS

Lobster Basics

Lobsters you buy today are, for the most part, smaller than those of yore. Recipes dating from the 1950s describe a "medium lobster" as weighing between one-and-one-half and two-and-one-half pounds, anything smaller being known as a "chicken lobster." Now, a medium lobster is one weighing from eighteen ounces to one-and-one-half pounds, and a chicken lobster weighs only a pound. From time to time, a picture will appear in one of the coastal New England newspapers showing a jubilant lobsterman hugging a deep-sea lobster almost as big as he is, but such Granddaddy lobsters are very scarce, and well warrant their pictures in the paper.

When planning a boiled or steamed lobster dinner, keep in mind that you'll need one medium lobster for each person, a quarter of a cup of melted butter, a slice of lemon, and a bowl for empty pieces of shell, along with lots of large napkins, a green salad, and plenty of French bread. Four 1½-pound lobsters can be cooked at once in a canning kettle, and each lobster will yield approximately one cup of meat.

You can buy whole lobsters either live or ready cooked. Needless to say, a live lobster is a dark, mottled green; a cooked lobster is "lobster red." Live lobsters should be active and aggressive as well as green. The tail of a properly cooked lobster should be curled up, and, when straightened out by hand and released, should promptly curl back up. Do not store live lobsters on ice (unless you are traveling with them); keep them in the refrigerator as you would fresh vegetables. Cooked lobster meat may be frozen, after removal from the shell.

Boiled or Steamed Lobster

Whether lobsters taste better boiled or steamed is a hotly contested question. As Cape Cod writer Margaret Koehler put it in her article "Seafood On and Off the Shell," in the July 1972 *Yankee* Magazine, "Cape Codders can argue about this little matter not just for hours but for years, and it is absolutely imperative to belong to one school or the other. If you subscribe to the boiling school, you fill a big receptacle full of boiling water, thrust your live lobsters into it, and boil them 20 minutes. Strangely, it doesn't seem to matter how much a lobster weighs when it comes to cooking time."

Even those who agree that boiled lobster is best cannot agree whether the water should be at a hard boil before the lobster is plunked (head-first) into it, or whether the lobster should be put into a pot of cold water, which is then brought to a boil, lobster and all, and then boiled for five minutes or longer. There is no doubt, however, that the water should be seawater if possible, or tap water to which one-third cup rock salt (or one tablespoon table salt) is added per quart of water, and that there should be enough water to cover the lobster(s).

While lobster-steaming adherents also use seawater or salted water, this method is "another kettle of lobster." As Mrs. Koehler said, "If you belong to the steaming school, you put about two inches of water into your big, deep receptacle, bring it to a boil, thrust your lobsters [head-first] inside and let them steam, also for 20 minutes.

"Devotees of the first [boiling] school maintain that lobster meat is more succulent when it is boiled and that steaming toughens it. The second [steaming] school maintains that lobster meat is more succulent when it is steamed and that boiling toughens it."

Regarding the necessity of using seawater (or salted water), Mrs. Koehler adds, "Probably I shouldn't admit it—but after several years of 'saltwater steaming' my husband forgot to go down to our landing to get the necessary solution when we were having guests for dinner one night, substituted regular tap water without saying anything, and I never knew the difference! In fact I seem to remember saying that those were the best lobsters I'd ever eaten—but then, I say that every time we have lobster."

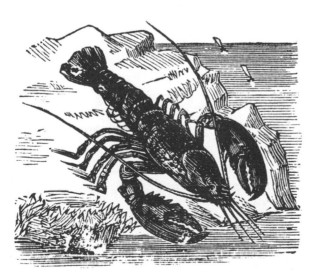

TO SERVE BOILED OR STEAMED LOBSTER

Remove boiled or steamed lobster from pot with a pair of tongs. Scrub shell with a vegetable brush under cold water to clean. Then turn lobster right side up, curl tail under, and place on serving plate with small dish of melted butter (¼ cup) and a slice or wedge of lemon.

TO DISMEMBER A LOBSTER

To extract the meat from a cooked lobster, turn the lobster on its back. Twist off the claws where they meet the body. Use a nutcracker to crack the shell of the claw, and separate the joints. Use your fingers, a lobster pick, or a sharp knife to poke the meat out of the joints. Crack the claws themselves enough so that you can get the meat out in one piece. Separate the tail from the body, break off and discard the flippers at the tip of the tail, then, with your thumb or a fork, push the meat up from the tip of the tail until it comes out the other (big) end. Remove and discard the black intestinal vein. Split the body shell in half up the back with a sharp knife. There is a small amount of meat in the cartilaginous crevices where the small claws are attached. You can remove some of this with a sharp-pointed knife. (There is a tiny bit of meat in the joints of the legs themselves, but if you are dismembering the lobster to use in another recipe it is not worth the time it takes to squeeze this out.) Besides the meat, take out the greenish tomalley and the pinkish roe sometimes found in the body cavity. Both are edible. Discard everything else.

BROILED LOBSTER

4 live lobsters
   (about 1½ pounds each)
1½ cups cracker crumbs
¼ teaspoon salt
2 teaspoons
   Worcestershire sauce
4 teaspoons melted butter
   Lemon slices or quarters
   Melted butter

Dispatching the lobsters is at best an unenviable task, but the end result is delicious enough to assuage the mental anguish involved. Broiled lobster is absolutely superb, and quite, quite different in taste from boiled.

For each live lobster, cross the large claws and hold firmly with left hand. Make deep incision with sharp, pointed knife at mouth of lobster and draw knife quickly through entire length of body and tail. Open lobster flat, butterfly-fashion, and remove and discard dark vein running down length of body. Remove and discard small sac lying at back of head. Scoop out the greenish tomalley, or liver, and surrounding liquor. Mix tomalley and liquor with cracker crumbs, salt, Worcestershire sauce, and 4 teaspoons melted butter. Set aside. Crack claws with nutcracker, and place lobster, shell side up, on preheated broiler. (Oven temperature set to broil, or roughly 550°F.) Broil 6–8 minutes, then take from oven, flip over, stuff cavity from which tomalley was taken with tomalley-crumb dressing, then return to broiler, stuffed side up, for 8–10 minutes. Serve at once, garnished with lemon slices and plenty of melted butter.

Serves 4.

LOBSTER THERMIDOR, MERCHANTS' LIMITED STYLE

The Merchants' Limited, and its earlier-scheduled twin, the Advance Merchants' Limited, were the New York Central's crack pair of commuter trains between Boston and New York City. Favorites of the Club Car set, these all-reserved-seat trains served delicious meals and covered the distance between the two cities in four hours flat.

2	cold boiled lobsters, whole
½	teaspoon minced onion
½	teaspoon chopped parsley
1	tablespoon melted butter
1	tablespoon flour
1	cup rich milk or half-and-half
½	teaspoon dry mustard
¼	teaspoon salt
	Few grains cayenne
½	cup sliced, sautéed mushrooms
1½	teaspoons sherry
	Grated Parmesan cheese
	Parsley for garnish

Remove head, claws, legs, and feelers from each lobster without splitting shell. Take poultry shears and cut out the bottom, or membranous side, of the tail. Withdraw meat and dice. Wash out shells. Sauté onion and parsley in butter until onion is golden. Blend in flour and gradually add milk or half-and-half, stirring constantly until sauce comes just to boiling point. Turn down heat and simmer for 2 minutes. Remove from stove and stir in mustard, salt, and cayenne. Add lobster, mushrooms, and sherry, mixing well. Fill each empty lobster shell with this mixture through opening in tail. Place, open side up, on baking sheet and sprinkle with cheese. Bake in middle of 400°F. oven for 10–15 minutes, or until heated through. Garnish with parsley.

Serves 2.

CRAB

Each pound fresh or frozen King crab legs will yield 1½ cups cleaned cooked crab meat. Put 1 quart water, 2 tablespoons cooking oil, and 1 tablespoon salt in a large kettle with a steaming rack on its bottom, and bring to boil. Break crab legs at the joints and add to kettle. Cover kettle and steam for 10–12 minutes. Take legs from kettle and slit lengthwise with scissors. The oil with which the crab was steamed softens the shell, making it easier to cut. Pull out the meat, which should come cleanly away from hard membrane. Remove any bits of membrane adhering to the meat.

CRAB NORFOLK

This excellent recipe found its way to New England from the Old South.

3 tablespoons butter
3 tablespoons flour
1 cup milk
½ cup chicken stock
3 tablespoons sherry
Dash cayenne
1½ cups cooked crab meat, membrane removed
1 cup sliced, sautéed mushrooms (or canned mushrooms, drained)
Cracker crumbs

Melt butter, blend in flour, and gradually add milk and chicken stock, stirring until sauce thickens. Add sherry and cayenne. Mix with crab meat and mushrooms and place in buttered 1½-quart casserole. Top with cracker crumbs. Bake at 375°F. for 20 minutes, or until cracker crumbs are browned and sauce is bubbling.

Serves 4.

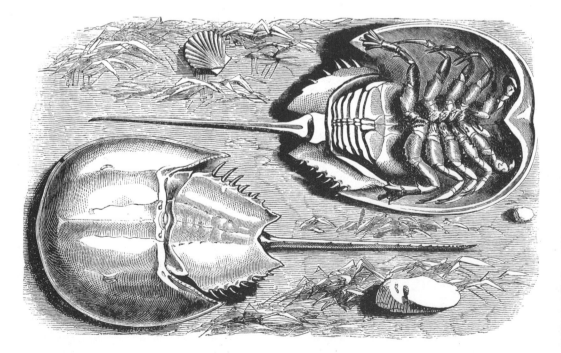

DEVILED CRAB MEAT

An equivalent amount of drained, flaked tuna can be used instead of crab meat here, for a less expensive, but almost as good dish. Serves five as an hors d'oeuvre, two or three as a luncheon dish with salad.

Drain crab meat, remove membrane, and shred. Melt 2 tablespoons butter, add flour, and stir to a smooth paste. Add milk gradually, and cook, stirring constantly, until sauce thickens and comes to a boil. Add mustard, parsley, salt, and Tabasco. Cool slightly. Dip out ¼ cup of sauce and add to egg in a thin stream, while stirring the egg. Return to rest of sauce and add crab meat and ½ cup bread crumbs. Toss remaining ½ cup bread crumbs in 1 tablespoon melted butter. Fill greased crab or scallop shells (or individual ramekins or custard cups) with crab mixture and top with buttered crumbs. Bake at 375°F. for 20–25 minutes.

Serves 3.

1 can (6½ ounces) crab meat
2 tablespoons butter
2 tablespoons flour
1 cup milk
1 teaspoon dry mustard
1 tablespoon chopped parsley
½ teaspoon salt
¼ teaspoon Tabasco sauce
1 egg, beaten
1 cup soft bread crumbs
1 tablespoon melted butter

SHRIMP

These little pink denizens of the sea are favorites coast to coast, thanks to sophisticated techniques for preserving and transport that allow one to purchase shrimp almost anywhere—fresh, frozen, or canned. Shrimp are available in sizes varying in diminishing order from jumbo to large, medium, and tiny.

To cook fresh shrimp, drop them, with or without shells, in boiling water. Turn down heat immediately and simmer shrimp for 3–5 minutes. Drain and peel off shells, if need be—a process akin to shelling a hard-boiled egg. Always be sure to remove the "black vein," equivalent to the mammalian intestinal tract. Pick off the vein with a toothpick or knife. The peeled-off shells, boiled in a little water, yield a tasty liquor. Frozen shrimp are usually sold shelled and de-veined. Drop in boiling water and boil for 2–3 minutes only (further cooking will toughen the shrimp). When this time is up, drain the shrimp in a colander and pour cold water through them to arrest the cooking process.

Canned shrimp, usually sold in cans similar in size to the seven-ounce tuna-fish cans, are labeled "4½ ounces, drained weight," the extra two-and-one-half ounces being brine. Canned shrimp are almost always smaller than the fresh or frozen varieties, but there is a real saving in buying cans of shrimp pieces, or shrimp which did not survive the canning process intact. Always drain canned shrimp and rinse in a colander or strainer a few minutes under cold running water.

SHRIMP ITALIAN STYLE

¼ cup dry sherry or
    vermouth
½ small clove garlic, split
½ cup fresh chopped
    mushrooms
1 teaspoon soy sauce
1 tablespoon oregano
2 cans (6 ounces each)
    tomato paste
1 cup water
2 cups cooked shrimp
    Salt and pepper

You can use fresh, frozen, or canned shrimp. Rinse and drain canned shrimp before using.

Combine first five ingredients and bring to boil. Stir in tomato paste and water, mixing well, and turn heat to low. Simmer for 10 minutes. Add shrimp and simmer for 5 minutes more. Remove garlic and season to taste. Serve over spaghetti or green noodles.

Serves 4.

NEW ORLEANS SHRIMP

1½ pounds raw shrimp,
    peeled and de-veined
    (reserve shells)
3 cups water
¼ cup butter
½ medium-sized onion,
    chopped fine
2 small green peppers,
    seeded, cut fine,
    and parboiled
½ bay leaf
    Pinch thyme
1 teaspoon salt
⅛ teaspoon black pepper
2 tablespoons cornstarch
¼ cup cold water
1 tablespoon soy sauce
3 tomatoes, peeled and
    cut into eighths

The stock achieved by boiling the shrimp shells in water is essential to the taste of this seductive Creole dish. Better not to try it with canned shrimp.

Prepare shrimp. Boil shells in 3 cups water to make stock for sauce. Melt butter and sauté shrimp and onion gently just until shrimp changes color. Add stock, green peppers, bay leaf, thyme, salt, and pepper. Let cook for 5 minutes. Thicken with cornstarch mixed to a paste in ¼ cup cold water. Add soy sauce and tomatoes. Heat gently 6–8 minutes or until the tomatoes are tender but firm. Serve with rice pilaf or plain rice.

Serves 6.

FISH

Trying to characterize *Fish*, in general, would be like trying to describe *Animals*—fish are not just something to eat, but a whole world of creatures whose lives are just as circumscribed by the natural rules governing their home environments of brook, pond, lake, river, sea, or ocean, as our own lives are. Nor can any cookbook, let alone a small section of one, devoted to "FISH" hope to include ways to cook every kind of fish in their manifold multiplicity. Here, we must confine ourselves only to some New England specialties, and to other superb fish recipes contributed over the years to *Yankee* magazine, recipes that are tried and true, and proven delicious.

The first recipe in this section—Court Bouillon—will be useful for all manner of fish recipes besides those included here.

COURT BOUILLON

Use for poaching fish.

Melt butter in skillet, add vegetables, and sauté for 5 minutes. Add remaining ingredients and boil for 5 minutes. Strain.

Makes 1 quart.

3 tablespoons butter
1 onion, chopped
1 stalk celery, diced
1 carrot, chopped
½ cup vinegar
2 sprigs parsley, chopped
1 quart boiling water
1 bay leaf
6 whole cloves
4 peppercorns

CAPE COD FISH PIE

1 box (1 pound) salt codfish
    fillets
2 tablespoons butter
2 tablespoons flour
2 cups scalded milk
1 hard-boiled egg, chopped
2 teaspoons lemon juice
    or vinegar
1 raw egg
3 cups freshly mashed, hot,
    unseasoned potatoes
    Salt and pepper to taste
    Pinch nutmeg
1 tablespoon chopped
    parsley

This venerable and justly renowned dish must be made with salt codfish, freshened, which the bland sauce and mashed potatoes complement nicely. (You can make lots of great dishes with fresh cod, but this is not one of them.) Serve with pickled beets (p. 91) and Indian pudding (p. 183) for a real, old-fashioned, Yankee meal.

Freshen the codfish as directed on the box, or as follows. First, cover fish with cold water and let stand for 4 hours. Drain off water. Next, cover with cold water, bring to a boil, and drain. Repeat the boiling and draining at least three times, or until fish tastes like fresh fish well seasoned with salt. Then, simmer fish in water for 10 minutes, or until fish flakes when broken. Do not boil the freshened cod at any point, or it will become tough. Drain, and set aside.

Melt butter and blend in flour. Add milk gradually, stirring to blend, and cook until sauce has thickened, stirring as needed. Add chopped hard-boiled egg and lemon juice or vinegar. Remove from heat. Arrange freshened cod fillets in greased 9-x-13-inch baking dish and pour the sauce over. Beat raw egg into mashed potatoes. Season to taste with salt and pepper, and stir in nutmeg and parsley. Spoon potatoes over fish. Bake at 350°F. for 15–20 minutes, or until heated through.

Serves 6–8.

BAKED BASS OR BLUEFISH

1 4-pound bass or bluefish,
    cleaned and split
4 strips bacon
¼ teaspoon freshly ground
    pepper
    Chopped parsley
    Lemon wedges

Easy to make and good with either fish; the sauce makes it very special.

Preheat oven to 425°F. Place fish, skin side down, in shallow oiled baking dish. Place bacon strips across it. Sprinkle with pepper. Bake uncovered until fish flakes easily when tested with a fork (20–25 minutes). Sprinkle lightly with parsley and serve with lemon wedges or cold Sour-Cream Dill Sauce (see below).

Serves 6–8.

Sour-Cream Dill Sauce

1   egg
1   teaspoon salt
     Pinch pepper
     Pinch sugar
4   teaspoons lemon juice
1   teaspoon grated onion
2   tablespoons snipped dill
1½   cups sour cream

Beat egg until fluffy. Add remaining ingredients, blending in the sour cream last. Chill.

CODFISH BALLS OR CAKES

Traditionally New England. As Mrs. Child, author of The Frugal Housewife, *printed in Boston in the 1830s, wrote: "There is no way of preparing salt fish for breakfast so nice as to roll it up in little balls, after it is mixed with mashed potatoes; dip it into an egg, and fry it brown." No one has disputed her to date. Codfish balls are Sunday morning breakfast, served with a dash of homemade tomato catsup or cranberry sauce, crisp bacon, and toasted brown bread.*

½	**pound salt codfish**
2½	**cups potatoes, diced**
1	**tablespoon butter or cream**
⅛	**teaspoon pepper**
1	**unbeaten egg**

Wash codfish and shred (don't cut) into small pieces to fill 1 cup. If fish is hard, soak it in cold water to cover for 4 hours or more. Drain. Put fish in saucepan with potatoes, cover with boiling water, and cook until potatoes are tender (about 10 minutes). Drain, return to stove, and leave uncovered for a few minutes to allow steam to escape. Remove from stove and mash thoroughly; add butter or cream, pepper, and egg. Beat vigorously until the mixture is light and creamy (an electric beater is grand for this). Drop by spoonfuls into deep, hot fat (385°F.) and fry brown (about 1 minute); drain on absorbent paper, and serve at once.

This same mixture may be formed into little cakes with floured hands, and browned on both sides in hot bacon fat in a frying pan. Or, if you prefer, it may be cooked spread evenly over bottom of frying pan, in fat tried out from diced salt pork. Pour off excess fat and use dice for garnish. Cook until a crusty brown on the bottom. Fold like an omelet, and serve on a hot platter. The mixture may be prepared the day before cooking. Serve with scalloped tomatoes (p. 99) and/or crusty French bread for a delicious meal.

Serves 4.

BROILED SCROD

2   **pounds fresh fillets
    of scrod**
Melted butter
Salt and pepper
Lemon

A scrod is usually taken to be a young cod or haddock. For what else it may be, or may have been, see below. Serve with hashed brown or creamed potatoes for a traditional Yankee meal.

Preheat broiler to 500°F. Brush broiler rack or baking pan with melted butter. Place scrod on rack or in baking pan. Brush with melted butter, sprinkle with salt and pepper, and broil for 10–15 minutes. Take from oven, garnish with parsley, and serve with lemon.

Serves 4.

Scrod—A Controversy, but a Delectable Fish

by Robert X. Perry

My childhood days were spent on the Boston waterfront. My dad was the owner and founder of Perry's Sea Food, a retail fish market in South Boston close to Boston's once famous fish pier. One of the things that always fascinated me was my father's reaction to the many questions which the customers put to him as he prepared their orders. Few knew the difference between cod and haddock, fillet of sole and flounder—but *scrod* was a complete mystery. A story he used to tell customers on Mondays, and other "quiet" days, was about "Boston scrod." Most people in those days (and today as well) believed that there was such a fish. This, of course, is untrue. Father's story went like this:

"A fishing schooner would work the Grand Banks for ten days or so, catching fish every day that the weather would permit. The first day's catch would be gutted and iced down in the bottom of the fish hold, and each following day's catch would be added until the vessel was full. Then, under full sail, she would speed to the Boston Fish Pier where the catch would be auctioned off.

"Boston's famous Parker House did not desire to serve the fish that came out of the bottom of any ship's hold. This would be the oldest fish, flabby and soft from the weight of each succeeding day's catch on top of it. No, sir, the Parker House wanted only the choice, small, firm fish on the top layer of the hold—the *freshest*.

"It was impossible, however, for the Parker House's maître d' to predict what fish would be on the top layer. 'So who cares,' he thought. 'I must get tomorrow's menu to the printer tonight. If I print the menu with haddock and the top layer is cod, I might get away with it in Kansas City—never in Boston.' What to do? The answer was simple: he coined a name for a new seafood, *scrod.* 'We can serve scrod every day of the week,' he reasoned, 'and our clientele will know that they are getting the very best from the latest arrivals at the pier.' "

Haddock, cod, pollock, and hake are all related and all are caught off the New England coast. Only a real connoisseur can tell the difference (particularly between haddock and cod), if it's fresh from the ocean, properly prepared, and cooked without skin (fillets). In most cases Boston scrod in the old days would be either young cod or haddock, but one would never be quite sure.

I'm sure that this story will bring about a controversy regarding the derivation of the word *scrod.* Wherever I go, people express complete amazement when I advise them that scrod is a phony. The dictionary defines scrod as a noun as well as a verb:

I   SCROD—or Escrod
   1. a: a young cod. b: the young of any of several other fishes
      (as haddock).
   2. a: a small cod split and boned for cooking. b. a fillet taken
      from the thick meat just ahead of the tail of a fish (as a
      cod, haddock, pollock).
II   SCROD—scrodded; scrodding; scrods; to split or fillet (a fish)
      for cooking.

—Excerpt from article originally titled
"What Exactly Is Scrod?" in August 1974 *Yankee*

BAKED HALIBUT WITH LOBSTER SAUCE

2 pounds halibut fillets
½ teaspoon salt
⅛ teaspoon pepper
2 tablespoons melted
 butter
1½ cups milk

Haddock can be successfully substituted for the halibut in this dish if you increase the oven temperature to 400° F., using the same cooking time.

Cut halibut into serving pieces and place pieces in buttered baking pan or 1½-quart casserole. Sprinkle with salt and pepper and brush with melted butter. Pour milk over fish and bake at 350°F. for 20 minutes, basting twice. Serve with Lobster Sauce (see below).

Serves 6.

Lobster Sauce

2 tablespoons butter
2 tablespoons flour
1 cup milk
1 egg yolk, lightly beaten
⅛ teaspoon salt
 Pinch pepper
1 tablespoon lemon juice
½ cup diced lobster meat

Melt butter and blend in flour. Stir in milk gradually and cook, stirring, until sauce thickens. Dip out about a half cup of sauce and pour in a thin stream into beaten yolk, stirring the yolk as you pour in the sauce. Return mixture to rest of sauce and mix well. Add salt and pepper, lemon juice, and lobster.

CASHEW-STUFFED RED SNAPPER

1 red snapper, 3½ to 4 pounds
 Lime juice
 Sherry
 Salt
½ cup diced celery
1 green onion, chopped
½ clove garlic, minced
6 tablespoons butter
2 cups day-old bread crumbs
1½ cups chopped cashew nuts
 Pinch of nutmeg
¼ cup dried parsley flakes
½ teaspoon grated lemon
 rind
⅛ teaspoon thyme
1 cup white wine
 Fresh parsley for garnish

Absolutely superb—a dish that looks and tastes out of this world. Use a striped bass or cod if you can't find red snapper.

Have the red snapper cleaned, beheaded, and boned, if possible. Sprinkle with lime juice and a little sherry and salt. Refrigerate for 2–3 hours. Sauté celery, onion, and garlic in melted butter until just limp—about 5 minutes. Combine bread crumbs, nuts, nutmeg, parsley, lemon rind, and thyme and mix with sautéed vegetables.

Take fish from refrigerator, stuff with bread-crumb mixture, and sew up. Place in greased 9-×-13-inch baking dish and pour wine over fish. Bake at 350°F. for 45 minutes, basting frequently. Remove fish to heated serving platter and garnish with fresh parsley.

Serves 4.

POACHED FOURTH-OF-JULY SALMON

All the ingredients of the traditional Fourth-of-July dinner are ready at about the same time—salmon, poached, as below, and served with egg sauce, baby green peas, small new boiled potatoes, freshly baked rolls, and strawberry shortcake.

1 3-pound chunk of salmon
2 quarts boiling court bouillon (p. 55)
2 cups Egg Sauce (see below)

    Wrap salmon in cheesecloth and place in pot. Pour boiling court bouillon over fish and simmer over low heat for 25 minutes (or about 8 minutes per pound). Drain, lift out of pot, remove cheesecloth and skin, and pour Egg Sauce over salmon. Garnish with parsley.

Serves 6.

Egg Sauce

Melt butter and blend in flour. Gradually add milk, and cook, stirring constantly, until sauce thickens. Add chopped eggs and season.

4 tablespoons butter
4 tablespoons flour
2 cups milk
2 hard-boiled eggs, diced
   Salt and pepper to taste

SHAD

The shad, like other anadromous or river-spawning fish (salmon, eels, alewives, even some bass) all but disappeared from the upper Connecticut River from the time of the construction of the first dam, at Holyoke, Massachusetts, in the 1850s. In 1940, a fish ladder was constructed for the dam, but the fish ignored it, and died attempting to swim up the face of the dam. Newer fishways, constructed since, have little by little succeeded in bringing New England's nomad fish back to the Connecticut. The first managed to ascend the river in the 1950s. Predictably, these bold individuals were caught and stuffed for their pains. Nevertheless, the Connecticut is now once again open to the River Runners. In 1980, a record 160 salmon were verified returns to the river, and 375,000 shad.

PLANKED SHAD WITH ROE SAUCE

**A 3-pound shad,
  boned and split
Salt
Freshly ground pepper
  to taste
Melted butter**

The planked shad suppers held in Essex (the first Saturday in June) and Old Saybrook (early May), Connecticut, draw hundreds of shad-eaters annually. A buttered baking sheet can be used instead of the plank.

Oil an oak or hickory plank and heat it in a 450°F. oven. Arrange the shad, skin side down, in the center. Sprinkle with salt and pepper and brush well with melted butter. Bake 15 minutes, basting with butter. Reduce the oven temperature to 350°F., and bake 10 or 12 minutes longer, or until the fish is lightly browned and flakes easily when tested with a fork. Serve with Creamed Roe Sauce.

Serves 6.

Creamed Roe Sauce

3	**pounds roe**
3	**tablespoons butter**
1	**teaspoon chopped shallot**
1½	**tablespoons flour**
⅓	**cup cream**
2	**egg yolks, beaten**
	Salt, pepper, lemon juice
½	**cup buttered bread crumbs**

Parboil (see Sautéed Roe, p. 63), drain, dry, and mash the roe. Melt butter, add shallot, and cook 5 minutes. Add roe, sprinkle with flour, and add cream gradually. Cook slowly 5 minutes. Add egg yolks gradually and season highly with salt, pepper, and lemon juice. Spread over shad, and cover with bread crumbs. Bake in 400°F. oven until crumbs are brown. Garnish with parsley.

SHAD ROE

This reddish "extra dividend" of the female shad is a delicacy often termed "the American caviar." Serve it alone, or with its parent fish, or make it into a superlative sauce (see p. 62) to serve with shad. But always, no matter how you choose to use it, parboil shad roe first. For all the recipes below, the roe must be either parboiled or steamed first. You need one pair roe to serve two persons.

To Parboil Shad Roe

Prick roe with a fork all over and plunge into boiling water to which a little lemon juice (1 teaspoon) or white wine (1 tablespoon) has been added. Simmer about 10 minutes. Drain and dry.

Or prick roe as above and place in skillet containing ½ inch boiling water into which a little lemon juice (see above) or white wine (see above) has been added. Bring to a boil, cover, steam 10 minutes, drain, and dry well.

Sautéed Roe

Coat parboiled roe with seasoned flour, and sauté for 10–15 minutes in melted butter until brown on both sides (turn once). Sprinkle with lemon juice or white wine and serve garnished with crisp bacon strips.

STUFFED BAKED BUCK SHAD

1   **4-pound buck shad,
      cleaned and boned**
      Salt
¼   **cup butter**
1   **cup chopped onion**
½   **cup thinly sliced celery**
4   **cups bread crumbs**
¼   **teaspoon each thyme,
      rosemary, and tarragon,
      or ½ teaspoon sage**
2   **tablespoons lemon juice**
      Melted butter
1   **or 2 strips bacon**

A buck shad is the male; the female is known as a "roe shad." Now that shad can be commercially sold boned, shad fishermen no longer throw the boney buck shad "to the fishes," i.e. use them only as bait.

Sprinkle shad inside and out with salt. In a skillet, melt ¼ cup butter, add onion and celery, and cook until almost tender. Mix with bread crumbs, seasonings, and lemon juice. Stuff shad loosely with mixture and close with skewers and string. Place on a foil-lined baking dish. Brush shad with melted butter and place bacon over top. Bake at 350°F. until fish flakes easily, about 35–40 minutes. Baste with butter as necessary. Serve with lemon.

Serves 6.

SMELT

Some facts about these small, narrow, silvery fish whose white and delicate flesh can become quite addicting—as one Yankee puts it, "Fifteen lake smelt are just about right to serve one hungry fisherman." For a big man, he's about right. Ocean smelt, which are what you buy in the market, are between eight and ten inches long, whole; lake smelt are only about four to five inches long, though a Granddaddy, or "Jack" lake smelt, can be as large as the average ocean smelt. On the average, when smelt are to be part of a regular meal, with vegetables, a starch, and a dessert, serve three or four ocean smelt per person. Fresh-caught, they are delicious just pan-fried in butter; or, with smelt bought in the market, cook as below.

BROILED SMELT

Clean, rinse well, and wipe dry 12 whole smelt. Brush with melted butter and roll in flour seasoned with a little salt and pepper and 2 tablespoons snipped chives (*or* in seasoned corn-meal, no chives). Preheat broiler to 500°F. Arrange smelt in shallow, greased baking dish and broil about 4 inches from the heat for 10–15 minutes, basting with melted butter twice during that time. Turn once. Serve garnished with lemon quarters, one to squeeze over each fish.

Serves 3–4.

4

EGGS, CHEESE, AND ASSORTED CASSEROLES

Eggs and Cheese

Here are some different ideas for breakfast, brunch, lunch, or quite meatless supper. Did you know that they deviled or stuffed eggs two hundred years ago, just as we do today? The Welsh Rabbit is the real McCoy—not just cheese sauce on toast.

REDDING RIDGE CHEESE CUSTARD

Good just as is, though you can pass a tomato or mushroom sauce with it. Use instead of potatoes for dinner, or with green salad for lunch.

Cook macaroni as directed on package and drain. Soak bread crumbs in hot milk and add to macaroni along with remaining ingredients. Mix all well and turn into greased 2-quart casserole dish. Set casserole dish in pan of hot water and bake 45 minutes at 350°F., or until custard is set. Test custard with a silver knife; when knife comes out clean, dish is done. Serve hot.

Serves 6.

1 package (8 ounces) elbow macaroni
1 cup fresh bread crumbs
1 cup hot milk
3 eggs, well beaten
1 cup diced cheese
1 tablespoon chopped green pepper
1 tablespoon diced pimiento
2 medium onions, diced
1 tablespoon chopped parsley
¼ cup melted butter

STUFFED EGGS WITH MUSHROOM SAUCE

12 hard-boiled eggs
3 large mushrooms, chopped
1 tablespoon minced onion
3 tablespoons butter
1 tablespoon chopped parsley
1 tablespoon prepared mustard
1 tablespoon lemon juice
 Salt and pepper to taste
2 packages (10 ounces each) frozen chopped spinach, cooked and drained
2 cups fresh bread crumbs
4 tablespoons melted butter

An excellent lunch or supper dish that dates way back—to 1776 at least! Easily halved.

Shell eggs and cut in halves lengthwise. Remove yolks and mash. Sauté mushrooms and onion in butter until tender. Drain. Add to yolks along with parsley, mustard, lemon juice, and salt and pepper. Fill halved whites with mixture. In buttered 9-x-13-inch baking dish, place spinach. Add 1 cup Mushroom Sauce (see below) and mix well. Spread evenly over bottom of dish. Place stuffed eggs in spinach bed, and cover with remaining mushroom sauce. Toss crumbs in melted butter and spread over top. Bake at 350°F. until heated through and bread crumbs are browned.

Serves 8.

Mushroom Sauce

4 tablespoons butter
12 sliced mushrooms
3 tablespoons flour
½ cup chicken stock
½ cup white wine
1 cup cream
½ teaspoon lemon juice
 Salt and pepper to taste

Melt butter and sauté mushrooms in it. Add flour and blend. Gradually stir in chicken stock, wine, and cream, stirring constantly over medium to medium-high heat until sauce thickens. Stir in lemon juice, salt and pepper, and blend well.

Makes about 3 cups.

The Big Cheese

In 1941, a memorial was unveiled at Cheshire, Massachusetts, a little town in the Berkshire Hills. The memorial read "Big Cheese 1754–1841; Dedicated by the Sons of the American Revolution, 1940." Above these lines is the plaque of Elder John Leland (1754–1841 being his life dates), who was chiefly responsible for the making of the gargantuan cheese as a gift to President Jefferson.

Leland suggested that each farmer from the Cheshire community donate the milk from one day's milking for the making of the cheese. They readily agreed, and on July 20, 1801, wagons and sleds from every direction arrived at the cider mill with their offerings. As a safety measure, the press was strengthened by hoops so as to take care of its unusually heavy burden.

One month was allowed for the cheese to press, and on August 20th, it was removed to a cheese house, where it was carefully watched and turned over daily as the cheese ripened.

Then came the Big Cheese's journey to Washington.

The giant cheese measured four feet, six inches in diameter and one foot, six inches thick. It was hoisted upon a sleigh, and with Elder Leland and a companion in charge, began the first leg of the journey. At Hudson, New York, the cheese was loaded onto a boat and transported by water to New York City. Then in a wagon, drawn by six horses, their bridles handsomely decorated with ribbons, the strange gift proceeded on its way overland to Washington.

On December 29, 1801, the great cheese, in perfect condition, reached its destination. Two days later, Elder Leland presented the huge gift to the President in the famous East Room of the White House, where a large crowd of public officials had gathered to witness the unique event.

Taking into his hands a large knife, Thomas Jefferson cut the first slice from the mammoth cheese, saying as he did so: "I will cause this auspicious event to be placed on the records of our nation and it will ever shine amid its glorious archives."

—Excerpt from April 1941 *Yankee*

WELSH RABBIT

1   tablespoon butter
1   cup beer
4   cups grated cheese
      (cheddar, Monterey
      Jack, or Colby)
2   eggs, beaten
½   teaspoon dry mustard
1   teaspoon Worcestershire
      sauce
¼   teaspoon salt
1   teaspoon paprika
      Dash Tabasco sauce
6   slices hot buttered toast,
      or 3 split English
      muffins,
      toasted and buttered

History suggests that "rabbit" was the original name for this venerable and still popular dish. The Victorians, however, who referred to human legs as "limbs" (and then only when necessary), and even went so far as to make petticoat covers for the "limbs" of their pianos, called it "rarebit." And indeed the dish has nothing to do with rabbit, and is a rare bit! Many of the cheddar cheeses available today give this rabbit an undesirably grainy texture; we therefore suggest using a smoother cheese, such as Monterey Jack or Colby. This Olde English equivalent of Swiss fondue should be served on toast points, with ham, bacon, or sausage on the side, or alone with a green salad.

Melt butter in double boiler top over boiling water. Add beer. When beer is hot, add cheese and stir until melted. Dip out about ½ cup of cheese and beer mixture and pour slowly, in thin stream, into beaten eggs, stirring constantly. Then pour egg and cheese mixture back into double boiler top with cheese and beer mixture, stirring well to blend. Add seasonings and heat through, still over boiling water. Do not cook directly over flame, or heat too long in double boiler, or eggs will curdle. Serve over toast or split English muffins.

Serves 6.

EMPRESS OMELET

For a luxurious Sunday breakfast in bed or Sunday night supper.

Omelet

Beat egg whites stiff. Beat yolks until thick and lemon-colored. Beat in hot water and salt and pepper. Fold in whites. Melt 3 tablespoons butter in skillet or omelet pan and turn pan so that sides are greased, too. Turn eggs into pan and cook over medium heat for 8–10 minutes, or until puffy and light brown underneath. Then bake in 350°F. oven for about 10 minutes, or until top is dry. As soon as top does not stick to finger when touched, it is done. Take omelet from oven and cover with filling (see below). Loosen edges of omelet with spatula, fold in half over filling, slip onto serving platter, and pour sauce (see below) over top. Serve at once.

Serves 3–4.

6   **eggs, separated**
¼   **cup hot water**
    Salt and pepper
3   **tablespoons butter**

Filling and Sauce

In 2 tablespoons melted butter sauté mushrooms. Add oysters, liquor, and chicken and cook gently. Season with salt and pepper. When oysters are just cooked, but still soft, cut them in half lengthwise. When omelet is ready, pour filling over top. Melt 1 teaspoon butter and blend in flour. Stir in ½ cup chicken stock and stir until sauce thickens slightly. Pour over filled, folded omelet before serving.

2   **tablespoons melted butter**
2   **mushrooms, sliced thin**
6   **fresh oysters**
3   **tablespoons oyster liquor**
4   **tablespoons cooked chicken meat, cut into mince or julienne**
    Salt and pepper
1   **teaspoon butter**
1   **teaspoon flour**
½   **cup chicken stock**

Assorted Casseroles

Just as pancakes and waffles are associated with maple syrup, casseroles bring to mind that time-honored New England institution—the Church Supper, still going strong. To visit a church supper—and anyone who happens to be in the area is always welcome—is to dispel the myth of the laconic, stand-offish Yankee. True, Yankees do not gush over a stranger any more than they do over their own. An unfamiliar face in a small town, though, does provoke lively curiosity on the part of folk who—by choice, mind—rarely visit the Big World outside their immediate locale. And the same new faces provoke delight on the part of local merchants, inasmuch as New England's economy, like Old England's, is based to quite a large extent on "visitors from away," "summer complaints," or "off-islanders."

Church supper dates are announced in local newspapers, on storefront placards, or on the community bulletin board, usually located near the post office or town hall. A supper is a lively affair, suffused with contagious communal zest, where the food is unfailingly good, and where, for three or four dollars per person, you can eat all you can hold.

A church (or town) near the sea may put on a clambake, or a special seafood supper, and an inland church supper may also have a specific menu—Bradford, Vermont, is famous for its game suppers; Rindge, New Hampshire, puts on a terrific roast beef supper; many towns are renowned for spaghetti dinners, or chicken pie or bean suppers—but in the main, the rule is pot-luck. Pot-luck suppers verify the adage "many hands make light work," depending as they do on members of the congregation to bring their specialties to the supper, be it casserole, salad, rolls, pie, cake, or pudding. Whereas for "menu" suppers, you sit down at a table and wait to be served—either by the church ladies or by boy or girl scouts—a pot-luck supper is always buffet.

Passing along the pot-luck table, which is groaning with choice dishes out of which you ladle your favorite-sized helpings, you may hear "regulars" ask, "Which is *Dottie's* tetrazzini?" or, "Are those *Charlotte's* beans?" or, on the second go-round—for desserts—"Did Blanche send a pie?" The ladies, and men too, who contribute regularly to the church supper menus are famous locally, and justly, for their own specific dishes. If, as a newcomer, you hear such a question, follow the lead! The dish in question is bound to be even better than the others.

Church suppers start early, usually at five or six o'clock, though most have a second sitting an hour later. Get there early, if you want to eat fast or sit with a bunch of family or friends.

At a well-attended church supper, if you don't get there bung on time, you'll have to stand in line for a spell and find a seat where you can. Sometimes that's the best, for even if you've lived in the same town for years, often you end up sitting with a stranger or almost a stranger. Keep in mind that eating has the first priority, but, as you are mopping up the juice or the last of the beans on your plate with a bit of bread or roll, *then* your neighbor will turn to you, and, replete, you chat about this and that, in between trips to the bountifully laden dessert table!

CALEDONIAN BEEF STEW

A classic beef stew with a gravy thickened by oatmeal, rather than flour. You would never notice the difference, except that because this is such a good *stew, you might ask how it was made.*

Brown meat on all sides in 2 tablespoons butter. Remove with slotted spoon to 2-quart casserole. Sauté onion, carrots, and (optional) turnip in remaining butter (add 1 tablespoon more if necessary) until onion is golden. Add, with butter, to casserole. Add rolled oats, bouillon, water, and pepper and bake at 350°F. for 3 hours. Then add potatoes and peas; check water level, and add more if necessary—usually about ½ cup at this point. Add ½ teaspoon gravy color (Gravy Master, or other such), and bake for 1 hour longer, again at 350°F. Refrigerate overnight, and reheat at 350°F. until bubbling, about 20–25 minutes.

Serves 4–6.

1	pound chuck or stew beef, cut in cubes
2	to 3 tablespoons butter
1	onion, chopped fine
2	carrots, diced
1	small turnip, sliced (optional)
4	tablespoons rolled oats
2	teaspoons instant beef bouillon, or 2 beef bouillon cubes
2½	cups water (or to cover)
⅛	teaspoon pepper
3	potatoes, peeled and cut into 1-inch dice
1½	cups frozen peas (a 10-ounce package is 2½ cups)
½	teaspoon gravy color

OLD ENGLISH STEAK AND ONION PIE

2　**pounds lean stew beef,**
　　cut in 1-inch cubes
　　Flour for dredging
　　Salt and pepper
6　**medium onions, sliced**
　　thin
3　**tablespoons melted butter**

Because this dish is steamed rather than baked, the English would define it as a "pudding," but to American eyes and taste, it looks and tastes like a pie. The suet top is very good—tastes like the bottom crust of a baked meat pie. The pie takes no time at all to put together, and, once it's put on to steam, can be left strictly alone for the 6 hours' steaming required (the water does not need replenishing if the kettle is tightly covered—aluminum foil crimped over does just fine).

Dredge beef lightly with flour and sprinkle with salt and pepper. Sauté onions in butter until just tender. In 1½-quart mixing bowl or deep dish, place alternating layers of beef and onions until dish is level full. Add water to about ½ inch from top. Prepare suet crust (see below). Place over top of bowl or dish of meat and onions, trimming to fit. Place piece of clean cheesecloth over pie, large enough to hang at least 2 inches over sides of bowl. Tie down with strong piece of clean twine, well secured, by wrapping around the bowl a couple of times. (Thin, insulated wire is good, too, as it can be twisted tight.) Place pie on rack in large kettle and add boiling water to a depth that comes 1–2 inches up side of bowl. Cover kettle and heat just to simmer, then turn heat very low. Allow pie to steam for 6 hours. Then serve with baked potatoes, or rolls, and a vegetable or salad.

Serves 6–8.

Suet Crust

¼　**pound cold or frozen beef**
　　suet, or 1 cup,
　　shaved and minced
2　**cups flour**
1　**teaspoon salt**
⅔　**cup milk**

Shave meat-free, all-white suet ("bird" suet works fine) with sharp knife into paper-thin slices. Then cut slices into very fine mince. Add minced suet to flour and salt and work with fingers until well combined. Pour in milk to make dough that "cleans the bowl," and roll dough to ¼-inch thickness. Use as specified above.

Did You Know . . . ?

How to "cut the devil's throat?"
Horace Reynolds told about it in his article
"Down East Dialects":

A fellow-guest at Mrs. Stahl's excellent table (over her steak and kidney pie) said, reminiscing about his early days in Nova Scotia, "We kids used to see who could throw a rock the farthest and who could cut the devil's throat." We almost jumped down his throat with the question, "What does it mean—'to cut the devil's throat?'" He told us it meant to throw a stone up high so it would enter the water without making a splash, pretty much the opposite of our old friend, skipping stones, another boyish pastime, in which a splash is the by-product of the skip.

Excerpt from January 1955 Yankee

BEEFSTEAK AND KIDNEY PIE

A dish that came to America with the earliest English colonists and remains a favorite. Economical, too.

1   clove garlic, chopped
2½   tablespoons butter
2   pounds lean rump steak, cubed, dredged with flour
4   lamb kidneys
1   cup boiling water
1   teaspoon salt
½   teaspoon pepper
1   tablespoon Worcestershire sauce
1   bay leaf
2   cups peeled, diced potatoes (approximately 1-inch dice)
5   small onions, peeled
1   tablespoon chopped parsley
2   tablespoons flour
¼   cup cold water
     Pastry for 1-crust pie

In heavy covered pan, sauté garlic in butter. Remove garlic from butter. Sear meat in butter. Skin kidneys and remove hard centers. Cut in quarters. Add to seared steak and brown lightly. Add 1 cup boiling water, salt, pepper, Worcestershire sauce, and bay leaf. Simmer covered for about 2 hours, or until meat is nearly tender. Add potatoes, onions, and parsley, and cook for 30 minutes more. Mix flour to smooth paste with ¼ cup cold water, stir into stew, and cook, stirring occasionally, until gravy thickens. Turn into 1½-quart casserole and cover with pastry crust. Pierce crust to allow steam to escape. Bake at 450°F. just until crust is done—10–15 minutes.

Serves 6.

ROAST BEEF AND EGGPLANT

This is for left-over roast beef, not ground beef. Used as directed, it is superb; used with ground beef, only so-so.

Slice eggplant into ½-inch slices. Salt each unpeeled slice, pile on top of each other, top with a moderate weight, such as a heavy plate, and let stand for about 30 minutes. Mix meat with onion, garlic, parsley, salt and pepper, nutmeg, and marjoram, blending well. Cut eggplant slices in quarters and brown in hot olive oil. In greased 2-quart casserole place alternate layers of eggplant and meat mixture, adding 1 tablespoon tomato soup to each eggplant layer. Pour remaining soup over top and bake at 375°F. for 25 minutes.

Serves 4.

1 **medium eggplant, unpeeled**
Salt
3 **cups chopped, cooked roast beef**
3 **tablespoons grated onion**
1 **large clove garlic, mashed**
2 **tablespoons chopped parsley**
Salt and pepper to taste
Pinch nutmeg
2 **teaspoons marjoram**
4 **tablespoons olive oil**
1 **can (10 ounces) tomato soup**

STEAK AND MUSHROOM CASSEROLE

4   cube steaks (about
      1 pound all told)
4   tablespoons butter
2   large onions, sliced thin
1   pound fresh mushrooms,
      sliced
1   can (10 ounces) cream of
      mushroom soup
1⅔ cups buttermilk
2   tablespoons chopped
      parsley
1   teaspoon salt
¼   teaspoon pepper
¼   teaspoon dry mustard
4   medium potatoes, peeled
      and sliced
1   tablespoon butter,
      cut into dots

A relatively inexpensive, hearty, and delicious meal with built-in potatoes. Works up easily.

Brown steaks on both sides in 4 tablespoons butter. Remove from pan and sauté onions and mushrooms in butter until tender. Take from skillet with slotted spoon and place in bowl. In another bowl, combine soup, buttermilk, parsley, and seasonings. In 2½-quart greased casserole, alternate layers of potatoes, onions and mushrooms, and steaks, pouring a little soup mixture over each layer. Last layers should be *not* potatoes, onions, steak (as other layers are), *but* onions, steak, and potatoes. Dot with 1 tablespoon butter and bake at 350°F. for 1 hour.

Serves 4.

SUNFLOWER PIE

Enough pie pastry
   for 2-crust pie
   (see p. 168)
1   pound ground beef
1   large onion, diced
¼   teaspoon sage or thyme
      (not both)
1   teaspoon salt
⅛   teaspoon pepper
1   pint cottage cheese
4   eggs, beaten until frothy
¼   cup grated American
      cheese
   Paprika

You can make this either as one large pie (in a 15-inch pie plate or a slant-sided deep-dish pie plate), or as two 8-inch pies. Good hot or cold.

Roll out pastry and fit loosely into baking container (see above), making a fluted edge to stand up around pan rim. Brown beef in skillet. Lift out and set aside to cool. Sauté onion in drippings. Add onion and drippings to beef, along with sage or thyme, salt, and pepper, and toss lightly with fork. Spread mixture evenly on bottom of unbaked pie crust. Spoon cottage cheese over meat. Pour eggs gently over cottage cheese. Sprinkle grated cheese over all. Shake paprika to make pattern of petal-like ovals from center to edge of pie. Bake at 400°F. for 20 minutes, then reduce heat to 350°F. and cook 35–40 minutes more. Cut in wedges, one "petal" each.

Serves 6–8.

FLAKY-CRUST MEAT LOAF

Makes a party dish out of plain old meat loaf.

Roll out pastry dough to 11-x-18 inches. Blend beef with bread crumbs, onion, salt, pepper, and Worcestershire and tomato sauces. Turn meat out on dough and pat into shape of a loaf. Fold dough up over the sides of loaf, bringing together at top center. Fold ends as if wrapping a package, and moisten with cold water to seal the edges together. Out of pastry scraps, cut desired shapes—like flowers—to decorate crust. Brush with egg white. Cut slits to permit steam to escape. Place loaf on ungreased cookie sheet. Bake at 400°F. for 50–60 minutes. Serve hot with brown gravy, or with tomato or mushroom sauce.

Serves 6.

Pie pastry for 2-crust pie
1 pound ground beef
½ cup fresh bread crumbs
2 small onions, finely chopped
1 teaspoon salt
⅛ teaspoon pepper
1 teaspoon Worcestershire sauce
¼ cup tomato sauce
1 egg white

SWEDISH APPLE MEATBALLS

A pippin of a meatball, served in an easy and delicious sauce you'll find useful for other dishes as well.

Mix meats with bread crumbs, applesauce, eggs, onion, and seasonings. Chill, then form into small balls. Brown in skillet. Make gravy (see below). Put meatballs into gravy and simmer for 35 minutes, or until cooked through.

Serves 6.

1 pound ground beef
½ pound ground veal
½ pound ground pork
1 cup soft bread crumbs
1 cup warm applesauce
2 eggs, beaten
1 medium onion, grated
1 tablespoon steak sauce
2 teaspoons salt
½ teaspoon mace
¼ teaspoon allspice
Dash pepper

Gravy

Melt butter and blend in flour. Add bouillon gradually, and stir until smooth and thickened. Add celery leaves and meatballs.

¼ cup butter
¼ cup flour
2 cups bouillon
Few celery leaves

Origin of the Hamburger

by John Burnham

This tremendously popular, hearty sandwich originated in New Haven, Connecticut, in 1900. The scene was Louis' Lunch, a small lunch wagon located at 197 Meadow Street and operated by Louis Lassen, Sr. Louis' grandson and the current proprietor of the family business, Kenneth C. Lassen, describes how the hamburger was a by-product of his grandfather's popular thinly sliced steak sandwich.

"The trimmings of his steak sandwiches were ground up into hamburger and taken home to his family to be eaten. You can imagine the progression—more steak sandwiches, more by-products. Finally, the problem became acute, and the logical solution was to sell the by-product at its source. He broiled his hamburger patties with a thin slice of onion in the same broiler he used for his steak sandwiches, and placed them on a plate with some home-fries. However, by solving one problem, another was created—it took too much time to make a 'Hamburger Plate.' Grandfather's customers solved this problem for him: 'Hey, Louis, put that hamburger on two pieces of toast and let me get out of here.' Completely by accident and without realization, the hamburger sandwich was born in Louis' in the year of 1900."

—Excerpt from article originally titled
"The First Hamburger Sandwich," in May 1974 *Yankee*

TOURTIÈRE

The famous Canadian pork pie. Serve hot, with or without additional gravy (passed in a gravy boat), with vegetables or salad; or serve cold, as a delicious and transportable slice of lunch.

1 onion, chopped
2 tablespoons butter
1 pound lean ground pork
1 teaspoon salt
½ teaspoon pepper
¼ teaspoon nutmeg
½ teaspoon ground cloves
¼ teaspoon cinnamon
2 teaspoons cornstarch
1 cup water
Pastry for 2-crust pie (see p. 168)

Sauté onion in butter until golden. Add meat and cook over medium heat, stirring, until cooked through. Remove from heat and stir in salt, pepper, and spices. Mix cornstarch with ¼ cup of the water, then stir in the remaining ¾ cup water. Pour water into meat and mix well. Line an 8-inch pie pan with pastry and pour in meat mixture. Add top crust. Pierce in several places to allow steam to escape, and bake on cookie sheet in 425°F. oven for 10 minutes. Then reduce heat to 350°F. and bake another 30 minutes, or until crust is golden brown.

Serves 4–6.

BERLA'S PORK GRAVY

Serve over baked potato for a rib-sticking meal. Takes a real Yankee to appreciate this! Also known as "potato bargain."

½	**pound salt pork, diced**
2	**tablespoons flour**
1¼	**cups cold water**
4	**hot baked potatoes**

Fry diced salt pork in heavy skillet until pieces have produced about 2 or 3 tablespoons fat. Stir in flour to make a stiff ball, and fry this flour mixture until it is very brown—"scorched," as Berla says. This scorching gives the gravy its special flavor. Very gradually stir in cold water to make a smooth, thick brown gravy. Spoon liberally over split baked potatoes.

Serves 4.

SAUSAGE ROLL

Nicely flavored, quick, and easy.

2	**pounds bulk sausage**
2	**cups diced raw apples**
2	**small onions, diced**
2	**cups dry oatmeal**

On waxed paper, pat the sausage into a flat rectangular shape, about 20-x-12 inches, about ½ inch thick. Mix the apples, onions, and oatmeal, and spread over sausage. Roll like a jelly roll, tucking the edges in. Place in a baking dish in a 350°F. oven until done (about 45 minutes).

Serves 6–8.

HAM AND OYSTER SCALLOP

Serve this dish with unusual Creole dash for brunch, lunch, or dinner over toast points.

1 tablespoon chopped
   onion
2 tablespoons chopped
   green pepper
¼ cup butter
¼ cup flour
1¾ cups warmed milk
¼ cup oyster liquor
¼ teaspoon salt
2 cups cubed, cooked ham
½ pint drained oysters
1 cup fresh bread crumbs
2 tablespoons melted
   butter
   Paprika

Sauté onion and green pepper in ¼ cup butter until tender. Add flour and blend. Gradually add milk and oyster liquor. Cook gently, stirring, until thick and smooth. Add salt and ham. Pour into greased 8-x-8-inch pan. Top with oysters. Toss bread crumbs with 2 tablespoons melted butter and cover dish with buttered bread crumbs. Sprinkle with paprika. Bake at 350°F. for 25 minutes.

Serves 4.

BAKED HAM HASH WITH CHEESE SAUCE

A really tasty ham dish, less bland than ham loaf.

½ cup fine graham cracker
   crumbs
½ cup soft bread crumbs
⅔ cup milk
2 eggs, beaten
3 cups ground ham
1 small onion, minced
2 tablespoons chopped
   parsley
   Pinch pepper
¼ cup packed brown sugar
1 teaspoon Worcestershire
   sauce

Soak crumbs in milk and add to beaten eggs. In large bowl combine remaining ingredients, then add milk and egg mixture. Stir vigorously or work with hands to mix well. Place in greased 8-inch round cake pan and bake at 375°F. for 30 minutes or until slightly set. Serve with cheese sauce (see below).

Serves 4.

Cheese Sauce

¼ cup butter
2 tablespoons flour
2 cups milk
1 cup shredded cheddar
   cheese
½ teaspoon salt
¼ teaspoon Worcestershire
   sauce

Melt butter and blend in flour. Gradually add milk, stirring and cooking until thickened and smooth. Stir in cheese, salt, and Worcestershire, and continue to cook and stir until cheese has melted. Keep warm, if necessary, in double boiler.

Makes about 3 cups.

CHICKEN CHARTREUSE

A chartreuse originally referred to a mixture of meat and vegetables masked in jelly or aspic, served to the vegetarian order of monks of the Chartreuse monastery in France (famous for the yellow-green liqueur of the same name still made there). One of the order's chefs, in the nineteenth century, invented this way covertly to include meat in the monks' diet. An excellent way of re-presenting left-overs in an attractive form, this chartreuse molds the meat and vegetables in rice.

Cook rice and line bottom and sides of buttered 1½-quart mold with it, reserving ½ cup rice. Melt butter and blend in flour. Gradually add milk, stirring, until thickened. Stir remaining ingredients into sauce. Pack into mold atop rice. Pack reserved rice on top. Cover mold tightly with buttered paper, tied on with string, or crimped-on foil. Place mold in pan of hot water and steam in 375°F. oven for 30–40 minutes. Unmold and serve with mushroom (p. 66) or tomato sauce.

Serves 4.

⅔ cup raw rice
2 tablespoons butter
2 tablespoons flour
1 cup milk
1 teaspoon Worcestershire sauce
1 cup diced cooked chicken
½ cup dry bread crumbs
1 teaspoon paprika
1 tablespoon chopped parsley
½ teaspoon salt
1 tablespoon chopped onion
½ cup chopped celery

BASIC CURRY

A classic curry contributed by an English Yankee reader brought up in India in the days of the British Raj (Raj means rule). Use with any left-over meat or with hard-boiled eggs.

Mix onions and garlic. Sauté in oil until onions are tender. Stir in flour and curry powder. Cook gently, adding a touch more oil if necessary. Add apple. The longer you cook, stirring, at this stage, the less chance of curry tasting raw; be careful not to scorch mixture. Add tomatoes, and other ingredients except meat. Simmer for 20 minutes. Add meat and simmer 20 minutes more before serving. If curry gets too dry, add a little more stock or water. Serve over rice.

Serves 4.

3 onions, coarsely chopped
2 cloves garlic, chopped fine
2 tablespoons olive oil
2 tablespoons flour
2 tablespoons curry powder
1 apple, peeled, cored, and thinly sliced
2 tomatoes, peeled and chopped, with juice
1 teaspoon salt
1 teaspoon sugar
1 tablespoon coconut
½ cup raisins
1 tablespoon chutney
1 teaspoon lemon juice
2½ cups (about) stock (use beef stock for beef or lamb; chicken stock for pork, veal, or eggs)
1 pound cooked meat or chicken, or 6 hard-boiled eggs

3   tablespoons butter
2½ tablespoons chopped
      onion
3   tablespoons flour
½   teaspoon salt
¾   cup milk
¾   cup chicken broth
½   cup shredded sharp
      cheese
2   tablespoons sherry
¼   cup chopped green pepper
      (optional)
1½ cups diced cooked
      chicken
½   cup diced cooked ham
1   cup quartered cooked
      scallops (about ¼
      pound)
1   can (4 ounces) sliced
      mushrooms, drained
      and diced
1   tablespoon pimiento,
      diced

SCALLOPED PARTY CHICKEN

Scallops make ham and chicken taste just marvelous. Serve with 4 cups hot, fluffy, cooked rice.

Melt butter and sauté onion in it until golden. Blend in flour and salt. Combine milk and chicken broth and add gradually. Cook, stirring, until thickened. Add cheese and continue to stir until cheese has melted. Add sherry. Stir in other ingredients and heat through.

Serves 6.

2   cups minced cooked
      chicken
4   unbeaten egg whites
½   teaspoon salt
¼   teaspoon pepper
      Dash nutmeg
1   tablespoon chopped
      parsley
½   cup heavy cream
2   tablespoons chopped
      parsley

HOT CHICKEN MOUSSE

Stylish and smoothly textured.

Combine chicken and egg whites and stir to make a smooth paste, crushing chicken with back of spoon. Add seasonings and 1 tablespoon parsley, then gradually stir in cream. Sprinkle 2 tablespoons parsley on bottom of buttered 8-inch mold, 4-x-8-inch loaf pan, or 4 custard cups. Pour in chicken mixture. Cover with waxed paper or foil to prevent burning. Set mold, pan, or cups in pan of hot water and bake for 30 minutes at 350°F. (check cups at 20 minutes), or until mousse is firm. Unmold carefully and serve with mushroom (p. 66) or tomato sauce.

Serves 4.

SUNDAY CHICKEN HASH

Chicken and potatoes hashed in cream with mushrooms and liberally flecked with parsley.

Sauté onion and mushrooms in butter until tender. Add potatoes and chicken and cook until potatoes are slightly browned, turning from time to time. Stir in cream and parsley and heat through. Garnish with almonds and serve.

Serves 2–4.

½ onion, chopped
½ pound mushrooms, sliced
2 tablespoons melted butter
3 small potatoes, peeled, boiled, and diced
2½ cups chopped, cooked chicken
⅓ cup heavy cream
¼ cup parsley
2 tablespoons toasted almonds

CHICKEN OR TURKEY TETRAZZINI

A favorite way of dealing with left-over chicken or turkey, and a church supper standby.

Melt 4 tablespoons butter and stir in flour until well blended. Gradually add chicken broth, stirring constantly until thickened. Add white wine and cream and season to taste. Stir in mushrooms, chicken or turkey, and peas. In 3-quart buttered casserole, place half the noodles or spaghetti. Add half the chicken mixture and toss to mix. Repeat with the remaining noodles or spaghetti and sauce. Mix bread crumbs, 1 tablespoon melted butter, cheese, and almonds if you include them, and sprinkle over top. Bake uncovered at 350°F. for 40 minutes or until heated through and browned on top.

Serves 8–10.

4 tablespoons butter
3 tablespoons flour
2 cups chicken broth
4 tablespoons white wine
1 cup cream
Salt and pepper to taste
1 cup sliced, sautéed mushrooms (or canned, drained)
3 cups diced, cooked chicken or turkey
1 cup cooked peas, or fresh uncooked garden peas
3 cups cooked noodles, or 3 cups cooked spaghetti (broken up into pieces before cooking)
¼ cup dry bread crumbs
1 tablespoon melted butter
¼ cup Parmesan cheese
¼ cup slivered, blanched almonds (optional)

Heigh Ho—The Magical Fair!

by Linda MacNish

No other event can bring such a tingle of blushing excitement to the rosy cheeks of little children, or build such a steady fire of purpose and spirits in the hearts of young people, or light such a twinkle in the eyes of the still young-in-heart. There is nothing quite like visiting it; there is nothing even remotely like being involved in it. You'll find it in towns and villages all over the country: The County Fair.

If you've never prepared for a fair, you'll just have to imagine the weeks of planning that go into it: the weeding, the sewing, the canning, feeding the chickens—and the final, head-long rush as opening day gets near.

You wash the chickens' feet with a brush and a sponge, cut a batch of beans into exact half-inch lengths for canning, and pull up a bed of carrots to find three that are exactly alike; you stay up far into the night before the fair, ironing the wrinkles out of the bathing suit you just finished sewing, and you wind up with an orgy of baking.

Your family is incredibly tolerant; for days they have munched their way through pies that burned, muffins with air holes, and baking powder biscuits that would make good anchors; they eat all the rejects, and it probably takes several batches of rejects before the perfect pie, the beautiful muffins, the fluffy biscuits are chosen to carry the colors into battle.

The night before the fair opens to the public is like old home week to the exhibitors. You run into friends from 4–H camp, kids you haven't seen since the county dress revue, and acquaintances you made at the last fair.

Ever so gently you move the chickens from their crate into the display cages, and with great pride fasten the tag with your name on it; you've fed them, watered them, tended them all year—and now it's their turn to do you proud.

In the 4–H building, you hang up the bathing suit that just yesterday was a rumpled heap of cloth on your sewing machine; today it's a candidate for a blue ribbon and the chance to go on to The State Fair.

You arrange the carrots on a paper plate with all the artistry at your command, with never a thought about the number of carrots you pulled out of the ground; the family will eat them before they spoil. And on the shelves for baked goods go your muffins, your biscuits, your pie, with a little prayer that the judges will get to them before they're full from tasting the gooey tarts and prune danish somebody had the audacity to put there first.

—Excerpt from September 1971 *Yankee*

CHICKEN PIE

Classic New England, church-supper, and just plain all-American fare. No one can quite agree on whether this pie is best served with a biscuit or a pastry topping. There are a hundred and one versions. Here's ours.

Try out salt pork or cook bacon until just crisp. Remove with slotted spoon and place on bottom of 2½-quart casserole. In fat, sauté onions and mushrooms until tender. Add onions and mushrooms to potatoes, carrots, spinach, and chicken, and toss to mix all well. Pour Deluxe Sauce over and mix again. Pour into casserole dish on top of salt pork or bacon. Now, *either* bake in 350°F. oven for 45 minutes, or until bubbling, then top with baking powder biscuit rounds, turn oven to 450°F., and bake 15 minutes longer, or until biscuits are browned; *or* before placing in oven, top with pastry crust, prick to allow steam to escape, and bake pie at 350°F. for 50–60 minutes or until crust is golden brown.

Serves 6–8.

¼	cup diced salt pork, or 4 slices bacon
4	small onions, chopped fine (or 1½ medium onions)
½	cup fresh (or canned, drained) sliced mushrooms
4	medium potatoes, cooked and diced
3	medium carrots, sliced and cooked
½	cup cooked chopped spinach
2	cups cooked, diced chicken
	Deluxe Sauce (see below)
	Baking Powder Biscuits (p. 118) or Plain Pastry (p. 168)

Deluxe Sauce

Melt butter and blend in flour. Mix wine with broth and add gradually, stirring. Add cream similarly, and continue to stir until sauce begins to thicken. Dip out ⅓ cup sauce and add in thin stream to beaten egg, stirring. When well mixed, stir back into rest of sauce. Stir in seasoning and herbs. Pour over chicken and vegetables in casserole.

4	tablespoons butter
4	tablespoons flour
1	cup unsalted, dry white wine
1½	cups chicken broth
1	cup heavy cream
1	egg, beaten
1	teaspoon salt (omit if you use bouillon cube to make broth)
⅛	teaspoon pepper
¼	teaspoon tarragon or thyme
¼	teaspoon sage
1	tablespoon parsley

CASSEROLE OF ROAST DUCK

1 **duckling**
  Salt and pepper
1 **onion, diced**
1 **large carrot, sliced**
1 **stalk celery, sliced**
1 **bay leaf**
  Pinch thyme
6 **tablespoons melted butter**
3 **slices bacon, minced**
6 **pearl onions**
2 **pounds shelled peas**
½ **head lettuce, shredded**
  (use inner half)
½ **teaspoon salt**
1 **teaspoon sugar**
2 **cups water**
¼ **cup butter**

Duck cooked as directed here is a rare treat—never greasy. No table carving is necessary, nor are additional side dishes needed. Hot rolls go well with this casserole.

Season duck with salt and pepper. Prick skin all over with fork, and place on rack in roasting pan, breast side up. Bake at 425°F. for 15 minutes. Pour off fat. Turn breast down on rack and bake 15 minutes more. Pour off fat. Turn oven down to 325°F., remove rack, turn breast up, and roast for 1 hour and 20 minutes longer. After the first 20 minutes, add onion, carrot, celery, bay leaf, and thyme to pan and return to oven. Melt butter and cook minced bacon; brown pearl onions in the mixed fats. Add peas, lettuce, ½ teaspoon salt, sugar, water, and butter. Cover and cook for about 30 minutes. Take duck from oven, and with shears or a sharp knife, cut in half through breastbone and backbone. Cut each of these halves in two with a slanting cut between the ribs to separate wing and leg. Surround on heated platter with vegetables.

Serves 4.

5

VEGETABLES AND VEGETABLE PICKLES

Vegetables

You've heard 'em. They say it all the time, in that pinched (but firm) voice that isn't at all apologetic: "Oh—I'm not much for vegetables, really." And then they add plaintively, "Well, you see, my mother always cooked them to death and they were just like mush, had no taste at all. . . ." Then you serve them a sparkling new vegetable dish, cooked in a very simple but delectable way, and they say in innocent wonder: "What's this? It's really good!"

The cardinal rule in cooking vegetables is to cook them *only* until tender-crisp. That way they'll keep their shape and their flavor, and will not become mushy; texture is a very big factor in whether people like vegetables or not. Observing this rule usually assures the second rule, which is to preserve the color, so that vegetables look attractive when served. Serve two vegetables of contrasting colors on the same platter once in a while. And finally, don't hesitate to add companionable herbs, spices, and sauces.

The Land of the Bean

by Sinclair Hitchings and Barbara Veneri

1909 was the all-time boom year for beans in Boston. That was the year *The Bean Pot,* a journal of gossip, commentary, and poetry, offered itself to Boston readers. It proclaimed itself "A Boston Magazine for Boston Men." Its editorials, pursuing the bean-pot metaphor to the fullest, referred to each issue as "a baking" and urged readers to "dip in."

In their third issue, the editors asserted that "nothing but fresh Beans, corn-fed Pork, limpid Molasses and a rich brown Pot are employed in the editorial bakery."

From the previous issue of this same authoritative message to the world came the opinion that there is no official recipe for Boston Baked Beans. However, "real" Boston Baked Beans are navy beans artfully cooked with pork and molasses. *The Bean Pot* mentions an occasional onion buried in the bubbling beans, but never tomatoes. The mystique of Boston Baked Beans calls for a Boston bean pot, a traditional serving to all hungry gatherers at the supper table on Saturday night, and a big enough baking to ensure that beans are left over for Sunday morning breakfast.

Independent evidence exists to show that the popularity of beans in Boston was at its height in 1909.

The Bean Pot, available for "A Dime the Copy" and "A Dollar the Year," survived only through September. At various spots in Boston, however, there were other graphic and literary testimonials to the bean. Postcards dated as early as 1906 and as late as 1911 sing the praises of Boston beans with a fervor and color which has never been matched, before or since.

They associated baked beans with pulchritude, motherhood, and childhood, not to mention Boston culture. The link between literature and beans, forged so energetically in the pages of *The Bean Pot,* is pictured on a postcard showing a Boston belle who rests one hand on a steaming bean pot, the other on a huge volume of Browning.

—Excerpt from article originally titled
"Browning, Brown Bread and Boston Baked Beans," in November 1972 *Yankee*

LAKE MONOMONAC BAKED BEANS

A true slow-baked flavor with carefully blended spices to add that extra touch; the fragrance while they are cooking may entice the neighbors in.

Sort beans carefully; put in water to cover and soak overnight. Bring to a boil in same water, adding more if necessary, and simmer gently until tender, about 1½–2 hours. Drain, reserve liquid. Cut salt pork in half and score both halves; make cuts ½ inch deep. Spread a layer of beans in a 4-quart bean pot or casserole dish, and put half the salt pork in. Mix onions, parsley, and thyme, and spoon some over the beans. Mix mustard, brown sugar, ginger, optional baking soda, salt and pepper, and molasses, and add some of this mixture on top of onions. Repeat layers until all ingredients are used; end with bean layer. Add reserved cooking liquid, and enough boiling water to cover beans. Place remaining salt pork on top of beans. Cook, covered, for 6–8 hours in 275°F. oven. Uncover during last ½ hour of cooking.

Serves 12–14.

2	pounds yellow eye beans
¾	pound salt pork
2	onions, sliced
¼	cup parsley
½	teaspoon dried thyme
2½	teaspoons powdered mustard
½	cup brown sugar
1	teaspoon ginger
1	teaspoon baking soda (optional)
1½	teaspoons salt
	Pepper to taste
½	cup molasses
	Boiling water

HOT CRANBERRY BEANS

Easy and delicious, this different vegetable dish stars the Vermont cranberry bean.

Soak dried beans overnight in water to cover. Simmer beans in 1½-quart saucepan, using soaking water and additional water to cover, for 2 hours, or until tender. Sauté green onions and celery in oil until just tender and add parsley; combine with beans. Add salt and pepper to taste.

Serves 4.

1½	cups dried cranberry beans
6	scallions and green stems, chopped
½	cup chopped celery
⅓	cup olive oil
½	cup chopped parsley
	Salt and pepper

CARROT CASSEROLE

A colorful go-with for fried chicken, pork chops, or beef.

Combine carrots, eggs, cheese, onion, salt and pepper, and paprika. Add butter and mix well. Pour into a greased 1½-quart casserole. Bake at 325°F. for 40 minutes.

Serves 4.

2	cups cooked, mashed carrots
3	eggs, beaten
2	cups grated cheese
1	small onion, minced or grated
	Salt and pepper
	Paprika
2	tablespoons butter, melted

SUCCOTASH SUPREME

2 cups corn kernels
1½ cups fresh or frozen
baby lima beans
½ cup boiling water
½ teaspoon salt
½ teaspoon sugar
2 ounces salt pork
3 tablespoons melted
butter
2 teaspoons flour
2 tablespoons light cream
¾ cup corn liquid or water
Salt and pepper
Dash curry

Making this old-fashioned favorite from scratch using fresh ears of corn adds a delectable sweet flavor that is well worth the trouble, and cooking the limas with salt pork makes them tender as can be. The dash of curry adds definite class.

Boil 10 ears of corn 5 minutes, then split the kernels down the middle of each row, and scrape kernels and milk off the cobs to make 2 cups. Or use 2 cups drained, canned niblets, reserving liquid for later use. Put lima beans in boiling water; add ½ teaspoon salt, sugar, and salt pork. Cook until almost tender. Combine beans and corn in 2-quart saucepan, adding butter, flour, cream, and corn liquid or water. Simmer until hot. Add seasonings.

Serves 6.

CAULIFLOWER WITH SHRIMP SAUCE

2 heads cauliflower
(2 pounds each)
2 tablespoons lemon juice
Water to cover stems
2 teaspoons salt
1 can cream of shrimp soup
½ cup light cream
½ cup tomato juice
Dash cayenne

Show off whole cauliflower heads served in this delicate sauce in an attractive low vegetable dish or platter.

Trim leaves and stems from cauliflower heads, and wash thoroughly. Make 2 gashes, ½ inch deep, across stems; brush tops with lemon juice. Place cauliflower, stem ends down, on rack in shallow roasting pan. Add enough water to just cover stems. Add salt to water. Bring to a boil, then turn down heat, cover, and steam gently for 40–45 minutes, or until tender. Meanwhile, put soup in medium saucepan; stir in cream and tomato juice, add cayenne, and bring to boiling, stirring frequently. Keep warm. Drain cauliflower; place in heated serving dish. Spoon sauce over top.

Serves 8–10.

ROYAL BROCCOLI CASSEROLE

2 cups cooked, chopped
broccoli
1 large onion, chopped
2 tablespoons butter
1 teaspoon salt
¼ teaspoon tarragon
or marjoram
⅛ teaspoon pepper
1 pint sour cream

Quick and easy way to make broccoli into "Something royal."

Place broccoli in buttered 1-quart casserole dish. Sauté onion in butter till soft and add to broccoli. Add remaining ingredients and blend well, smoothing top. Cover and bake in 325°F. oven for 25 minutes.

Serves 4.

PICKLED BEETS

The classic accompaniment to Cape Cod Fish Pie (p. 56). Canned beets may be used, but freshly cooked ones are infinitely better. Good cold, too.

Combine sugar, water (or canned beet juice), and salt in a 1-quart saucepan and boil for 5 minutes. Add vinegar, beets, and cinnamon. Bring back to boil and simmer until heated through.

Serves 4–6.

½ **cup sugar**
½ **cup water (or liquid drained from canned beets)**
¼ **teaspoon salt**
¼ **cup vinegar**
2 **cups sliced beets, freshly cooked and drained (if you use canned beets, drain and reserve ½ cup juice to use in place of water)**
Dash cinnamon

HOT CABBAGE-APPLE SLAW

Just what any good Yankee—or anyone else—would want on a cold wintry day. Good flavor with a tang of tarragon.

Wash cabbage and put in 2-quart saucepan along with vinegar, sugar, butter, tarragon, and salt and pepper. Bring to a boil, then stir in apple. Cook gently until apples are hot.

Serves 6.

3 **cups cabbage, shredded**
3 **tablespoons vinegar**
1 **tablespoon sugar**
2½ **tablespoons butter**
2 **teaspoons minced tarragon**
Salt and pepper
2 **medium-sized apples, grated**

GREEN BEANS IN GRAPEFRUIT SAUCE

A new idea to try with those friendly old green beans . . . may make a difference next time company comes.

In double boiler top, melt butter over low heat with Tabasco and onion. Stir in undiluted grapefruit concentrate and heat. Serve warm grapefruit sauce over cooked beans. Garnish with optional grapefruit sections.

Serves 6.

4 **tablespoons butter**
¼ **teaspoon Tabasco sauce**
1 **tablespoon grated onion**
6 **tablespoons (3 ounces) grapefruit juice concentrate, thawed, undiluted**
2 **packages (10 ounces each) frozen whole green beans, cooked and drained, or 4 cups fresh green beans, cooked and drained**
Sections from 2 grapefruits (optional)

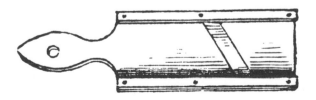

Memories of My Hull-Corn Man

by Barbara Whitney Woods

One of my earliest and dearest memories takes me back to the days of "Hull-Corn Bowen." I may have coined the name. If older people did use the term, it was due to small town vernacular and with no sense of disrespect. Surely there was nothing but adoration in my young heart, and I waited by our driveway each Thursday afternoon with fingers firmly clasped about the handle of my little blue mug.

My old friend hulled his own corn and delivered it in person. He was a spare man with a long gray beard, and invariably wore a long gray duster. He drove a droopy looking black horse hitched to an ancient buckboard. A huge weather-worn box with a slanting top was fastened back of the seat. This held quantities of freshly hulled corn and a tin measuring dipper. I have forgotten what he charged per quart for his product, but I do remember that every Thursday directly after dinner my mother put the correct change in a large white bowl and placed it on the kitchen table where it would be "ready." The corn that went into my little mug cost nothing at all. That was always a good will offering from one friend to another.

—Excerpt from January 1941 *Yankee*

CORN CUSTARD

2 cups fresh corn kernels, or canned, drained niblets
1 tablespoon sugar
2 tablespoons flour
½ teaspoon cornstarch
¾ teaspoon dry mustard
3 eggs, well beaten
2 cups milk
1 tablespoon Worcestershire sauce
2 tablespoons melted butter

A creamy corn custard that goes particularly well with baked ham or roast chicken.

Mix the corn and dry ingredients together. Add eggs, milk, Worcestershire sauce, and butter, and blend well. Bake in a 2-quart buttered baking dish or casserole set in a pan of hot water in a 350°F. oven for 50–60 minutes, or until a knife inserted into the center comes out clean. Do not overcook.

Serves 4–6.

To Prepare Fresh Corn on the Cob for the Freezer

Boil 3 quarts of water in canning kettle; place shucked ears in wire basket and suspend above the water. Cover the kettle and cook. When the steam begins to escape, cook for an additional 8 minutes, then remove ears *immediately* and chill for 15 minutes in ice water. Dry thoroughly with soft towel, then wrap each ear in plastic wrap and tape securely. (When corn on the cob is removed from the freezer for use, it should be thawed completely, then cooked in a small amount of boiling water 3–4 minutes, or until heated through.) A delicious lift for winter menus.

Vegetable Hint

A speedy way to super vegetables is to have a few pots of herb butter and your own mixture of *fines herbes* on hand. Add to fresh, frozen, or even canned vegetables to lift them right out of the ordinary.

HERB BUTTERS

Keep a few little pots of herb butter in your refrigerator for easy use. Just mix 1 tablespoon of any fresh herb, or 1 teaspoon dried herb, with ¼ pound of butter. (If you use dried herbs, add a bit of minced parsley or fresh, chopped spinach for color.) Cover tightly and label; use as desired.

FINES HERBES

Most *fines herbes* mixes use four herbs. A typical *fines herbes* mix is composed of tarragon, chives, chervil, and parsley. Experiment, and mix your own. Try it on carrots, beets, string beans, peas, or cabbage. And of course, in omelets.

EGGPLANT AND TOMATO DISH

1   medium-sized eggplant, peeled or unpeeled, sliced
    Salt
4   large ripe tomatoes, peeled and chopped
2   cloves garlic, crushed or minced
1   cup olive oil
    Salt and pepper
1   teaspoon brown sugar
½   cup dry bread crumbs
½   cup grated sharp cheese

Good and interesting combination of flavors and textures; excellent with pork or chicken.

Sprinkle eggplant slices with salt on both sides; let stand 30 minutes. Meanwhile, simmer chopped tomato and garlic in 3 tablespoons of the olive oil until tomatoes cook down; add salt and pepper to taste. Mix sugar, crumbs, and cheese in bowl. Rinse eggplant slices in cold water and pat dry. Roll each slice in crumb mixture, then sauté until tender in remaining olive oil. Place a layer of eggplant slices in well-buttered 2-quart casserole dish; then add tomato sauce and crumbs. Repeat until all is used, topping with bread crumb mixture. Bake in 350°F. oven for about 30 minutes, or until top is browned. Good hot or cold.

Serves 4–6.

GREEN PEAS WITH LETTUCE

An interesting way to combine two of summer's tenderest vegetables.

Wash and drain green peas and lettuce. Season peas with salt and pepper and sprinkle with mint. Force open each head of lettuce and fill with ½ cup of peas. Tie up the heads vertically and horizontally with string, like small packages, and place on rack over boiling water. Cover and steam until peas are tender—about 30–35 minutes. When done, remove string gently, drizzle with melted butter, and serve in individual dishes.

Serves 4.

2 cups hulled green peas
4 small whole heads Bibb
   or other garden lettuce
   Salt and pepper to taste
⅛ teaspoon chopped mint
2 tablespoons melted butter

CUCUMBER AND EGGPLANT MEDLEY

Two old friends join forces in a colorful and flavorful casserole.

Sauté eggplant, cucumbers, onion, green pepper, and celery in butter until eggplant is nearly tender. Season with salt and pepper to taste. In 2-quart buttered casserole dish, alternate layers of eggplant mixture with tomato slices. End with eggplant layer. Add melted butter to cracker crumbs, mix well, and stir in cheese. Spread cracker mixture over top of casserole. Bake in 375°F. oven for about 40 minutes.

Serves 6.

1 small eggplant, peeled
   and diced
3 cucumbers, peeled,
   seeded, and diced
1 medium-sized onion,
   chopped
½ green pepper, chopped
½ cup diced celery
3 tablespoons butter
   Salt and pepper to taste
4 tomatoes, cut in thick
   slices
2 tablespoons melted butter
½ cup cracker crumbs
¼ pound grated cheese

WILTED GREENS

A fresh and tangy garden taste to add an accent to any dinner.

Wash greens well in cold water. Shake to remove most water. Put in serving dish. Melt butter in skillet and brown salt pork or bacon, and onion. Remove from heat and add vinegar. Mix well and toss with greens while mixture is still hot. Serve immediately.

Serves 4.

Raw young dandelion,
   endive, Swiss chard,
   or other greens
   (about 1½ pounds)
2 tablespoons butter
1 cup diced salt pork
   or bacon
1 small onion, coarsely
   chopped
¼ cup vinegar

EXTRA SPECIAL CREAMED ONIONS

A creamy mushroom sauce with nuts adds new zest to this traditional favorite, here baked with a cheese topping.

2   **pounds small white onions, peeled**
   Water
1   **tablespoon butter, cut up**
1   **can (10 ounces) cream of mushroom soup**
½   **cup light cream**
½   **cup chopped walnuts**
¼   **cup shredded American cheese**

Cook onions whole in lightly salted, boiling water until almost done (20–30 minutes). Drain. Place in buttered 1½-quart casserole. Dot with butter. Blend soup with cream and walnuts; pour over onions. Sprinkle cheese on top and bake at 350°F. for about 30 minutes or until cheese is melted and slightly browned.

Serves 4.

The Cellar That Had Everything

by Ruth Kirkpatrick Goodwin

To enter Grandpa's fruit cellar, one had to raise a large trap door that was on the west side of the kitchen. The cellar held more fruits and vegetables than any modern grocery store, and the selection was almost as great. Produce was not stored in boxes and baskets as some people stored their foods. Grandpa's cellar was divided into bins which were several feet square with partitions between them at least five feet high.

I don't know why it was always called the fruit cellar when it held about everything that needed to be stored in a place safe from freezing. There were bins filled with pears, potatoes, turnips, cabbage, pumpkins, beets, squash, onions, apples, and more potatoes, and more apples. Each gave forth an aroma that mingled with the others and seemed the very substance of life itself.

One corner of the cellar was reserved for our own produce, because Dad didn't have a fruit cellar. This always pleased me, because I had an opportunity to go to the cellar often and look at the bins and bins of vegetables and fruits and absorb some of their earthy aromas, and to pick out the reddest, largest apple.

The turnips that were stored in the cellar were not planted in the early spring with the rest of the garden. They were planted the 21st of July—wet or dry. Turnips never failed to produce in quantity if planted at the right time, Grandpa always said, and like the other vegetables, there was a wagon load year after year to be stored.

> —Excerpt from article originally titled "Grandpa's Fruit Cellar," in October 1957 *Yankee*

GLAZED PARSNIPS À L'ORANGE

Orange juice and parsnips are a particularly happy combination.

In a 1-quart saucepan, bring to boil parsnips, orange juice, sugar, salt, and spice. Cover and cook slowly until tender. Remove from heat and sprinkle with orange peel.

Serves 4.

1 pound parsnips, peeled and sliced ¼ inch thick
½ cup orange juice
1 teaspoon sugar
¼ teaspoon salt
Dash cinnamon (or allspice, or nutmeg)
Grated peel of 1 orange

PEPPERS STUFFED WITH TOMATOES AND SHRIMP

6 small or 3 large green
   peppers
1 small onion, chopped
1 small clove garlic,
   minced
1 tablespoon butter
1 teaspoon minced parsley
3 large tomatoes, peeled
   and chopped
1 teaspoon sugar
1 cup fresh bread crumbs
   Salt and pepper
1 egg, beaten
1 cup cooked fresh shrimp,
   or 1 cup canned shrimp,
   rinsed and drained
   Water

A superior summation of tasty parts.

Slice tops off small peppers, or split large ones. Seed peppers. Sauté onion and garlic in butter until golden. Add parsley, chopped tomatoes, sugar, and ½ cup bread crumbs; continue to sauté gently until all are cooked. Season, and stir in egg and coarsely chopped shrimp. Stuff peppers, sprinkle with remaining bread crumbs, and place in 8-x-8-inch baking dish with water to barely cover bottom. Bake in 350°F. oven for 25–30 minutes.

Serves 4–6.

CREAMED SPINACH DELUXE

2 packages (10 ounces each)
   frozen chopped spinach
   or 2 pounds fresh,
   washed and de-stemmed
⅓ cup boiling water
½ teaspoon salt
2 small packages (3 ounces
   each) cream cheese
   or 6 ounces
   Neufchâtel cheese
   Few grinds black pepper
⅛ teaspoon nutmeg
2 tablespoons butter
2 hard-boiled eggs,
   quartered

A quick way to superlative creamed spinach.

Cook spinach in boiling water with salt until just tender. Drain. Chop fresh cooked spinach fine. Place spinach in double boiler over boiling water. Add cream cheese, cut into 1-inch dice, and pepper, nutmeg, and butter. Cook in double boiler over simmering water until butter and cream cheese have melted. Stir vigorously to blend well. Serve garnished with hard-boiled egg quarters.

Serves 4.

SCALLOPED TOMATOES

An old favorite, perfect with sun-ripened garden tomatoes, and just as good made to use up tomatoes sliced for another occasion.

Simmer tomatoes, sugar, basil, parsley, and salt and pepper until tomatoes are tender. Add 2½ cups of the bread crumbs. Add olives. Pour into buttered 2-quart baking dish and top with remaining bread crumbs, cheese, and butter. Bake at 375°F. until topping is brown.

Serves 4–6.

3 cups raw, sliced tomatoes
2 teaspoons sugar
1 teaspoon basil
2 tablespoons parsley
Salt and pepper to taste
3 cups day-old bread crumbs
2 to 3 stuffed green olives, chopped
1 tablespoon grated Parmesan cheese
2 teaspoons butter, cut up

HASHED SQUASH

A fragrant and hearty vegetable dish; the touch of bacon is the distinctive ingredient.

Fry diced bacon in 2-quart skillet over slow heat until crisp, then add onion, cooking until golden. Add squash, tomatoes, green pepper, oregano, basil, and salt and pepper to taste. Cover and cook slowly until vegetables are tender, about 25 minutes. Stir from time to time to make sure all squash cooks evenly.

Serves 4–6.

3 slices bacon, diced
1 large onion, sliced thin
1 large or 2 small summer squash or zucchini, cut into 1-inch dice
2 cups peeled, chopped tomatoes
1 green pepper, chopped
⅛ teaspoon oregano
⅛ teaspoon basil
Salt and pepper

SWEET POTATO AND PINEAPPLE CASSEROLE

For the sweet-potato aficionado, a delectable concoction with ingredients to please the most incurable sweet tooth.

Boil potatoes or yams with skins on; when cool enough to handle, peel and cut into ½-inch slices. Layer sweet potatoes, spices, salt, and pineapple in a buttered 1-quart casserole. Top with marshmallows, and pour honey over all. Bake for 10 minutes at 400°F.

Serves 4.

6 small sweet potatoes or yams
⅛ teaspoon allspice
⅛ teaspoon ground cloves
⅛ teaspoon nutmeg
½ teaspoon salt
1 can (8 ounces) crushed pineapple with liquid
½ cup miniature marshmallows
½ cup honey

BRIANI

Zucchini, carrots, potatoes, onion, and tomatoes cooked and enhanced with wine and herbs.

1 onion, sliced
1 clove garlic, finely minced
¼ cup olive oil
3 carrots, scraped and
  thinly sliced
2 potatoes, peeled and sliced
2 medium zucchini,
  thinly sliced
2 large fresh tomatoes,
  peeled and chopped
¼ cup water
¼ cup white wine
1 teaspoon oregano
1 teaspoon basil
½ teaspoon cumin
  Salt and pepper to taste

Sauté onion and garlic in oil. Add carrots and potatoes and cook over medium heat about 5 minutes. Add remaining ingredients and cook covered over low heat until vegetables are tender, about 45 minutes.

Serves 4–6.

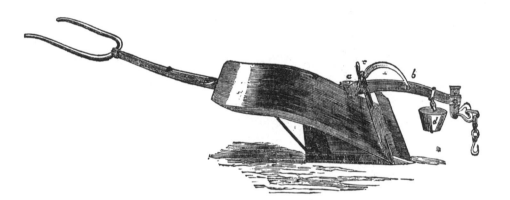

Vegetable Pickles and Relishes

"In a real pickle" is a great place to be should you happen to be a vegetable. Should you happen to be a pickle lover, you no doubt agree, with relish! No question but what good food becomes even better when served with just the right pickle or relish.

The Brining Crock

by Barbara Radcliffe Rogers

Sauerkraut, crisp sweet pickles, salted sweet corn, and a variety of dill-pickled vegetables are prepared entirely in a brining crock.

By "crock" I mean not only the stoneware or old pottery ones, but *any* unchipped enamel pot or large glass jar. One works just as well as another as long as the basic rules are followed. The gallon wide-mouth jars in which restaurants buy pickles are fine.

If you *do* have an old crock, and notice a white film inside that disappears when wet and reappears upon drying, don't use it for brining or pickling. It has been used for waterglassing eggs; there is no way to remove that coating, which will ruin your pickles.

The only magic rules in brining, apart from the strength of the brine, are to keep your hands and any metal object out of the crock. The old jingle "a hand in the pot spoils the lot" is true, and a metal spoon will do just as much damage. Use wooden spoons and mashers and glass or crockery for dipping or weighting.

—Excerpt from article originally titled
"Pickling and Brining Vegetables in a Crock," in July 1977 *Yankee*

AUNT MARY'S
APPLE PEPPER RELISH

Red, delicious, and different. Just the thing with ham; elegant with beef.

Put peppers, onions, and apples through coarse food grinder. Add lemon rind and juice and heat to boiling point. Add sugar and salt and boil, stirring as needed, until thick and syrupy (about 40 minutes). Fill hot sterilized jars; seal by covering with melted paraffin.

Makes about 2 pints.

4 sweet red peppers, washed, seeded, and cored
5 large sweet onions, peeled
6 cooking apples, peeled and cored
2 tablespoons grated lemon rind
⅔ cup lemon juice
2 cups sugar
2 teaspoons salt

MOCK WATERMELON PICKLES

Made with the ubiquitous zucchini!

Cut peeled zucchini in chunks. Heat alum in water but do not boil. Pour water over zucchini; cover with ice cubes and let stand for 2 hours. Drain. Combine 8 cups sugar, cinnamon sticks, vinegar, and cloves, and bring to a boil. Pour over drained zucchini and let stand overnight. Drain and reheat this syrup 3 mornings, adding an additional ½ cup sugar to syrup each time it is reheated. Pouring reheated syrup back over zucchini on the third day, boil up, pack into hot sterilized jars, and process in boiling-water bath for 10 minutes.

Makes 3 or 4 pints.

3	pounds zucchini, peeled
4	tablespoons alum
3	quarts water
	Ice cubes
8	cups sugar
4	cinnamon sticks
4	cups vinegar
4	teaspoons cloves
1½	cups sugar, divided

MOTHER'S MUSTARD PICKLE

A tangy mustardy sauce enhances seven colorful garden vegetables; adds zest to any meal.

Heat 4 quarts water to boiling, add salt, and dissolve. Pour over the vegetables, and leave overnight. In the morning, bring to boil and simmer vegetables until all are tender. Mix flour, mustard, turmeric powder, and brown sugar with enough cold water to make a smooth paste. Heat vinegar, add flour paste, and cook in a large kettle (6 to 8 quarts), stirring until smooth. Then add the vegetables, cloves, and cinnamon sticks. Bring just to boiling point, stirring as needed to heat evenly. Remove cinnamon sticks and cloves, and bottle in hot sterilized jars.

Makes 8–10 pints.

4	quarts water
2	cups pickling salt
1	quart sliced cucumbers
2	quarts sliced green tomatoes, cut up
1	quart small (button) onions
1	cauliflower, broken in small pieces
4	green peppers, chopped
4	red peppers, chopped
1	small bunch celery, cut fine
½	cup flour
4	tablespoons dry mustard
1	teaspoon turmeric powder
1½	cups brown sugar
	Cold water
2	quarts vinegar
4	whole cloves
2	cinnamon sticks

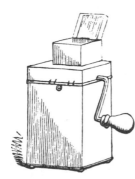

SLICED GREEN TOMATO PICKLE

The ultimate go-with for Boston Baked Beans . . . what else?

4 quarts green tomatoes, sliced thin, dry measure
1 quart onions, sliced thin, dry measure
1 cup pickling salt
2 red peppers, seeded and minced
4 sweet green peppers, seeded and minced
   Vinegar
12 whole cloves
   Handful stick cinnamon
1 teaspoon allspice
3 cups brown sugar
3 tablespoons mustard seed
3 tablespoons celery seed

Sprinkle tomatoes and onions with salt and let stand overnight. Next morning, drain off juice, rinse, drain, and rinse again to rinse out salt. Put tomatoes, onions, and peppers in canning kettle and just cover with vinegar. With cheesecloth, make a spice bag containing cloves, cinnamon, and allspice. Add to tomato mixture and cook until vegetables are soft. Remove spice bag; add sugar, mustard seed, and celery seed and cook 10 minutes more. Pour into hot sterilized jars and seal.

Makes 10–12 pints.

CARROT CHUTNEY

This economical version of its more exotic mango cousin is a pungent accompaniment for ham, pork, or curry, and a welcome variation for the chutney buff.

3   cups scraped and slivered carrots
½   teaspoon salt
½   cup boiling water
1½ cups liquid—carrot stock with water added to make up measure
2   cups sliced onions
1   cup seedless raisins
2   cups brown sugar
1   cup granulated sugar
1   cup cider vinegar
1   lemon, cut in half and sliced thin
1   teaspoon salt
½   teaspoon ground cloves
½   teaspoon nutmeg
½   teaspoon ginger
1   teaspoon cinnamon

Put carrots into salted boiling water, cover, and simmer until just tender. Drain off and measure carrot stock; add water as necessary to bring carrot liquid up to 1½ cups liquid. Return to pot and stir in remaining ingredients. Cook slowly until mixture thickens slightly (about 2½ hours). Put in sterilized jars and seal.

Makes 3 pints.

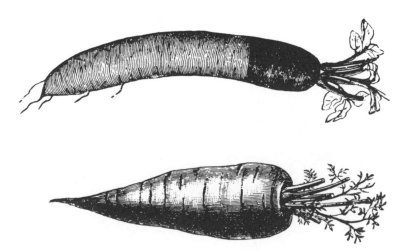

CORN RELISH

This colorful mixture has long been a great favorite.

Cut corn kernels from cobs but do not scrape ears. Mix together corn kernels, onions, peppers, and cabbage. Add remaining ingredients. Cook slowly for 1 hour, stirring occasionally. Pour into hot sterilized jars and process in boiling water bath for 10 minutes.

Makes about 5 half-pint jars.

12	ears sweet corn
2	onions, chopped
2	sweet green peppers, seeded and chopped
1	sweet red pepper, seeded and chopped
1	cup chopped cabbage
2	tablespoons pickling salt
¼	teaspoon pepper
1½	tablespoons dry mustard
1	cup sugar
2	cups vinegar

6

BREADS AND BREADSTUFFS

Yeast Breads

There is absolutely nothing better than fresh-baked bread to perfume your house, gladden your soul, or delight your family. Bread is in all truth the very "staff of life." The English title "Lady" derives from the Saxon word for the female head-of-house, meaning "bread-maker." Originally, the title owed its status to the importance of its owner in this capacity!

ANADAMA BREAD

This delicious bread was supposedly invented by a Massachusetts fisherman, weary of the same cornmeal-and-molasses porridge fixed by his lazy wife for supper every night. One night, resentfully muttering, "Anna, damn her!", he added flour, eggs, and yeast to the mixture, and put it into the oven. The resulting bread assuaged his anger.

Dissolve yeast in lukewarm water. Combine molasses, water or milk, salt, shortening, cornmeal, and 3 cups flour in bowl. Stir in yeast and stir mixture vigorously for several minutes to form a smooth dough. Work in remaining flour to form a stiff, non-sticky dough. Turn dough out on floured board and knead until smooth and elastic—about 10 minutes. Place in greased bowl, turning dough to grease top; cover, and let rise until doubled in bulk—about 1 hour. Punch dough down and let rest 10 minutes. Shape into 3 loaves, place in 3 greased 9-x-5-inch loaf pans, and let rise again until almost doubled. Bake at 350°F. for 35–45 minutes, until loaves test done. Cool on racks.

Makes three 9-x-5-inch loaves.

2 packages dry yeast
½ cup lukewarm water
⅔ cup molasses
2 cups water or milk, or 1 cup of each
1½ teaspoons salt
3 tablespoons shortening
1 cup cornmeal
7 to 8 cups flour

BANANA RYE BREAD

To lighten this unusual banana yeast bread, use half rye, half white flours.

Dissolve yeast in warm water. In bowl, combine salt, sugar, shortening, and banana. Add 2½ cups flour and beat until smooth. Beat in dissolved yeast. Stir in enough more flour to make a firm dough. Turn out onto floured board and knead until smooth, about 10 minutes. Place dough in greased bowl, turning to coat all sides of dough. Cover and let rise until doubled in bulk—about 1½ hours. Punch down dough and form into 2 loaves. Place in 2 greased 9-x-5-inch loaf pans, let rise until almost doubled, and bake at 350°F. for 35–45 minutes. Turn out on racks to cool.

Makes two 9-x-5-inch loaves.

2 packages dry yeast
3 tablespoons lukewarm water
1 tablespoon salt
1½ tablespoons sugar
3 tablespoons melted shortening
2¼ cups mashed banana (about 5 medium bananas)
5 to 6 cups rye flour (or 2½ to 3 cups rye flour and 2½ to 3 cups white flour)

Grains

In days gone by, New England farmers raised many kinds of grains on their farms—corn, wheat, rye, barley, oats—and threshed and had them ground locally. Most went to feed livestock, but some of each typically was used in the making of bread. This produced a variety of tastes and textures, and helped the cook get through the year—she could just use whatever flour she had left in the lean months without having to worry too much whether her bread would be edible.

OATMEAL BREAD

A moist bread, extra high in protein. Great with honey or peanut butter.

Dissolve yeast in 1 cup warm water. In separate bowl, combine oats, molasses, boiling water, salt, and lard or shortening. Let cool to lukewarm, and stir in yeast and 2 cups flour. Add enough more flour to make a kneadable dough. Turn out onto floured board and knead until smooth and elastic. Put in greased bowl, turn to grease all sides, cover, and let rise to double its original volume. Punch dough down and shape into 4 loaves. Place in 4 greased 9-x-5-inch pans, let rise until almost doubled, and bake for 15 minutes at 375°F. Turn oven down to 325°F. and bake 30–40 minutes longer. Turn out and cool on racks.

Makes four 9-x-5-inch loaves.

1 **package dry yeast**
1 **cup lukewarm water**
2 **cups rolled oats**
¾ **cup molasses**
4 **cups boiling water**
1 **tablespoon salt**
1 **tablespoon lard or shortening**
8 **to 10 cups flour**

RAISIN BREAD

A rich white bread laced with fat raisins and cinnamon.

Stir yeast and 1 tablespoon of the sugar into water. Combine milk, shortening, and 2 cups of the flour in bowl. Stir in yeast when mixture is lukewarm. Cover and let rise until doubled in bulk—1–1½ hours. Then add eggs, salt, remaining sugar, and remaining flour to make a soft dough. Cover and let rise again. Divide into two halves and flatten each half out. Sprinkle each with cinnamon and raisins and roll up to loaf-size. Place in 2 greased 9-x-5-inch loaf pans. Let rise until almost doubled. Bake at 375°F. for 40–50 minutes, until loaves test done. Turn out on racks to cool.

Makes two 9-x-5-inch loaves.

1 **package dry yeast**
¼ **cup sugar**
1 **cup lukewarm water**
1 **cup scalded milk**
2 **tablespoons shortening**
6 **cups flour**
2 **beaten eggs**
1 **teaspoon salt**
2 **teaspoons cinnamon**
1 **cup seeded Muscat raisins**

SALT-RISING BREAD

This bread won a prize over a hundred years ago. Although many find the method too time-consuming today, the end result is worth the effort. Lacking a wood stove, set yeast to rise in the morning, to bake at night.

Yeast

1⅓ cups warm water
1 teaspoon salt
½ teaspoon brown sugar
1 cup flour
2 teaspoons flour

Combine water, salt, brown sugar, and enough flour to make a thin batter. Set in double boiler over hot water or in warm place, cover, and let rise. Keep water in bottom of double boiler hot, but do not heat pan on stove. Stir in 1 teaspoon flour twice during fermentation. Leave overnight. In the morning, yeast should reach top of pan.

Bread

6 cups flour
  Yeast from above
1 quart milk, lukewarm
  More flour to make
    stiff dough

Sift flour into bowl and make well in center. Pour in yeast and milk and stir into sticky dough. Cover and let rise 1 hour. Add enough more flour to make stiff dough, knead until smooth and elastic, and shape into 4 loaves. Place in 4 greased 9-x-5-inch pans and let rise until almost doubled. Bake at 350°F. for 40–50 minutes. Turn out on racks to cool.

Makes four 9-x-5-inch loaves.

WHITE BREAD

A good basic recipe that can be altered in many ways. For example, add an egg or two and another cup of flour for a richer loaf; or substitute one cup soy flour for one cup of the white; or add one-half cup wheat germ.

1 package dry yeast
¼ cup warm water
1 cup scalded milk
1 cup water
2 tablespoons shortening
1 teaspoon salt
1 tablespoon sugar or honey
5 to 6 cups white flour

Stir yeast into ¼ cup warm water and let stand 5 minutes to dissolve. Combine scalded milk, 1 cup water, shortening, salt, and sugar in bowl and let cool to lukewarm. Stir in yeast mixture. Stir in 3 cups flour and continue stirring vigorously with spoon until dough is smooth. Work in 2 to 3 cups more flour to form stiff dough. Turn dough out on floured board and knead until smooth and elastic—about 10 minutes. Place dough in greased bowl, turning the dough to coat its top. Cover and set in warm place to rise until doubled in volume—about 1 hour. Punch down and shape into 2 loaves. Place in greased 9-x-5-inch pans and let rise again until almost doubled. Bake at 350°F. for 40–50 minutes, until tops are brown and loaves sound hollow when tapped.

Makes two 9-x-5-inch loaves.

PARKER HOUSE ROLLS

The *basic white dinner roll. Originated at Boston's famous Parker House Hotel, and still made and served there.*

2 cups milk
2 tablespoons butter
2 tablespoons sugar
1 teaspoon salt
1 package dry yeast
¼ cup warm water
5 to 6 cups flour
   Butter, softened

Scald milk and combine in mixing bowl with 2 tablespoons butter, sugar, and salt. Let cool to lukewarm. Dissolve yeast in warm water and stir into milk mixture. Stir in 3 cups flour and stir vigorously until dough becomes smooth. Work in 2 to 3 cups more flour until dough is soft but not sticky. Turn out on floured board and knead until smooth and elastic. Place in greased bowl, turn to grease all sides, cover, and let rise until doubled in bulk. Punch down and again turn out on floured board. Push and pat into rectangle ½ inch thick. Cut into rounds with floured biscuit cutter. Spread each round on one side only with softened butter, fold in half with buttered side inward, and gently pinch edges together. Place about 1 inch apart in greased baking pan, cover, and let rise until almost doubled. Edges will unseal as rolls rise. Bake in oven set at 350°F. for 15–20 minutes, until rolls are nicely browned. Serve hot.

Makes about 2 dozen rolls.

Read below and appreciate your own oven!

Baking in the Brick Oven
by J. Almus Russell

Once you are sure your oven is fireworthy, lay bark over the floor of the oven and lay the kindling "cob-housewise" over the bark. Lay old barrel staves or cleft hardwood over that, light the fire, and close the oven door. Let the fire burn for two hours, after which time the materials will be reduced to a bed of glowing coals. If the hair on a hand held just inside the oven is singed off, the oven is hot enough. Carefully remove the coals and sweep the hot oven clean of ashes. Now put slow-cooking foods to the rear of the oven, faster-cooking ones toward the front. Close the oven up again. After 45 minutes to an hour the first batch will be done and can be taken out to make way for the second.

—Excerpt from October 1939 *Yankee*

DILLY ROLLS

Dill seed and poultry seasoning blend to make this an unusually savory lunch or dinner roll.

Soften yeast in warm water. Combine with remaining ingredients, stirring to blend thoroughly. Turn out on floured board and knead until smooth, 2–3 minutes. Pinch off bits of dough and roll into 22 balls. Flatten slightly and place on greased cookie sheet so they don't quite touch each other. Cover with damp cloth and let rise until doubled in bulk, about 45 minutes. Bake at 400°F. for 15–20 minutes until nicely browned. Serve fresh from the oven.

Makes about 22 rolls.

1   package dry yeast
      (1 tablespoon)
¾   cup warm water
2½ cups flour
1   teaspoon salt
2   tablespoons shortening
2   teaspoons baking powder
1   teaspoon poultry
      seasoning
1   tablespoon dill seed

DARK YEAST ROLLS

Dense, nutritious, flavorful.

Combine milk and ¾ cup water in small pan and bring to boil. In bowl, mix shortening, oats, all-bran, salt, molasses, and sugar. Pour boiling liquid over them. Cool to lukewarm. Dissolve yeast in ½ cup lukewarm water and add to mixture in bowl. Stir in flour and blend thoroughly. Cover and let rise until doubled in bulk—about 45 minutes. Turn out onto floured board and knead until smooth. Form into walnut-sized rolls and place on greased baking sheet. Let rise until doubled in bulk—about 45 minutes. Bake at 425°F. for 20–25 minutes, until tops are browned.

Makes 24 rolls.

¾   cup milk
¾   cup water
½   cup shortening
½   cup rolled oats
½   cup all-bran cereal
1   teaspoon salt
3   tablespoons molasses
2   tablespoons brown sugar
2   packages dry yeast
½   cup lukewarm water
4   cups flour

NO-KNEAD WHOLE-WHEAT BREAD

A flavorful loaf with a dense texture, it takes its time to rise.

Put flour in bowl in warm spot so it will become slightly warm. Dissolve yeast in ½ cup warm water and stir in molasses. Combine yeast mixture, remaining water, oil, and salt with flour, and stir to make a sticky dough. Spoon into greased 9-x-5-inch loaf pan, making sure dough reaches into corners of pan. Put in warm place to rise. When volume has grown by about ⅓, bake in 450°F. oven for 30–40 minutes.

Makes one 9-x-5-inch loaf.

4   cups whole-wheat flour
2   packages dry yeast
½   cup warm water
2   tablespoons molasses
      or honey
1¼ cups warm water
¼   cup cooking oil
1   teaspoon salt

Quick Breads

Quick Breads are so called because they are quick to make, quick to rise, and quick to bake, thanks to baking powder or soda, whose one-time action begins upon contact with liquid, and is rapidly completed during baking. Baking powder is a fairly recent invention as cooking ingredients go, having been discovered in 1857 by Professor E. N. Horsford of Harvard. Until that point, quick breads were raised with "saleratus," or baking soda, mixed with buttermilk (or other acid ingredient); or they were raised using "pearlash," a refined form of potash. Should there be any doubt as to the value of Professor Horsford's invention, recall that among other things, baking powder financed one of the most successful racing stables in America—Calumet!

Brown Bread

Boston brown bread is as much a part of New England as cod or baked beans, and usually accompanies the latter. Made from cornmeal and molasses, those indispensable items of Yankee cuisine, this rich steamed bread can be cooked in the oven right beside the beanpot, and adds its smell to the spicy aroma of baking beans. Raisins can be added or not, as you like; but true brown bread always had them. They get plump and juicy during the steaming process, and gleam like dark jewels when the finished loaf is sliced.

Slice this bread hot from its steamer, using a piece of taut string to cut through it.

If all the brown bread was not eaten at one meal, Yankee thrift demanded that it be transformed and eaten another time. Leftover chunks were turned into Brown Bread Brewis (opposite page) and served up for breakfast or supper.

BROWN BREAD

Traditional verse passed through the generations of one Yankee family for more than 200 years:

2	cups cornmeal
1	cup white or rye flour
1	teaspoon salt
½	cup seeded raisins (optional)
2	teaspoons soda
2	cups sour milk or buttermilk
1	cup molasses

> *Two of meal, one of flour*
> *One of sweet, two of sour*
> *Two of soda, one of salt*
> *Boil three hours without a halt.*

In prose, it goes: Combine cornmeal, flour, and salt and mix thoroughly. Stir in raisins if used. Stir soda into milk, add with molasses to dry ingredients, and stir only enough to blend. Fill 2 well-greased 1-quart molds half full, cover tightly, and steam for 3 hours. Remove from steamer and take off covers immediately. Unmold and serve hot or cold with plenty of butter. Use a taut string to slice.

Serves 6–8. Makes 2 loaves.

BROWN BREAD BREWIS

Common to all the New England states, this dates from the earliest times, and is the height of thrift.

2	cups milk or light cream
1	tablespoon butter
1½	cups left-over Boston Brown Bread (see p. 114), broken into small bits
½	teaspoon salt

In saucepan, bring milk or cream and butter just to the boiling point. Stir in brown bread bits and salt, remove from heat, and let soak for 5 minutes. Then simmer gently until bread has absorbed all liquid—about 5 minutes. Serve hot, topped with butter or cream.

Serves 4–6.

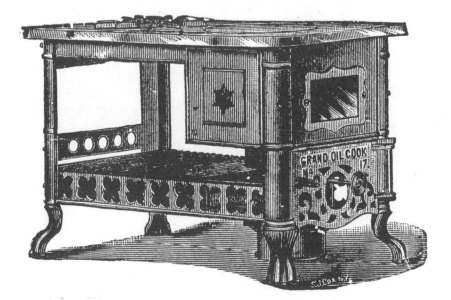

APPLESAUCE NUT BREAD

A high-rising, closely textured, cake-like bread. Use walnuts, pecans, or almonds.

1   cup sugar
1   cup applesauce,
       at room temperature
⅓   cup oil
2   eggs
3   tablespoons milk
2   cups flour
1   teaspoon baking soda
½   teaspoon baking powder
½   teaspoon cinnamon
¼   teaspoon salt
¼   teaspoon nutmeg
¾   cup chopped nuts

TOPPING
¼   cup brown sugar, packed
½   teaspoon cinnamon
¼   cup chopped nuts

Combine sugar, applesauce, oil, eggs, and milk, and blend thoroughly. In separate bowl, combine flour, baking soda, baking powder, cinnamon, salt, and nutmeg. Stir into applesauce mixture and blend thoroughly. Stir in chopped nuts. Pour into greased 9-x-5-inch loaf pan.

Combine topping ingredients and sprinkle over loaf, pressing topping lightly into batter. Bake at 350°F. for 30 minutes, then cover top loosely with foil. Bake 20–30 minutes more, until loaf tests done. Cool in pan for 10 minutes, then turn out and cool on rack.

Makes one 9-x-5-inch loaf.

Yankee Thrift

by J. Almus Russell

Mother used to make her own bread. Every week she set a sponge in a large iron-ware bread pan, placed on a small table behind the kitchen stove. One Friday evening, she set the sponge as usual, threw a clean remnant of a freshly laundered turkey-red tablecloth over the bread bowl, and retired for the night.

The next morning as we entered the kitchen, Mother glanced in the direction of the rising bread dough. Strangely enough, the tablecloth was not to be seen although the bowl still remained in its usual place and position. Then I discovered that Peter, the house cat, becoming chilly during the night, had jumped upon the bowl. His weight had gradually carried the cloth downward into the dough while the sponge had risen high around him, making a warm and springy mattress.

As ours was a thrifty Yankee family, Mother shooed Peter off the table-cloth, removed the covering, decided that no harm had been done, and baked the bread as usual.

—Excerpt from April 1939 *Yankee*

COLONIAL BREAKFAST BREAD

Serve this tangy bread warm. Colonials considered oranges a real treat, and the old Yankees always saved the peels.

Cream sugar, orange juice, and 1 tablespoon butter until light. Sift together flour and baking powder and stir orange peel into them. Add dry ingredients alternately with milk to creamed mixture, blending well after each addition. Bake in greased 8-inch- or 9-inch-square pan at 375°F. for 20–25 minutes. When done, spread top with 1 tablespoon butter and dust with combined sugar and cinnamon. Serve warm.

Serves 9.

1 cup sugar
1 tablespoon orange juice
1 tablespoon butter
2 cups flour
2 teaspoons baking powder
1 tablespoon orange peel
¾ cup milk
1 tablespoon butter
1 tablespoon sugar
1 teaspoon cinnamon

BAKING POWDER BISCUITS

The basic recipe. Use as biscuits, pie toppings, pizza crust, or dumplings. Quick to make and bake for hot bread at any meal.

2   cups flour
½   teaspoon salt
2   teaspoons baking powder
2   tablespoons butter
¾   to 1 cup cold milk
      or water

Sift together flour, salt, and baking powder. Cut in butter with pastry blender or 2 knives. Stir in liquid to form a stiff dough. Turn out on floured board and knead briefly. Pat out to ¾-inch thickness. Cut into rounds with floured biscuit cutter. Place close together on ungreased baking sheet. Bake 15–20 minutes in 400°F. oven, until tops are lightly browned. Serve piping hot with lots of butter.

Makes about 12.

LEMON BREAD

A rich, lemony loaf just right for afternoon tea. Aging these loaves after they have baked lets the flavors meld and the topping seep through and through.

1   cup oil
1½ cups brown sugar
4   eggs
½   teaspoon salt
½   teaspoon baking soda
1   cup buttermilk
3   cups sifted whole-wheat
      flour
      Grated rind of 3 lemons
1   cup finely chopped
      pecans

GLAZE
½   cup brown sugar
½   cup lemon juice

Combine oil and brown sugar and beat in eggs one at a time. Stir salt and soda into buttermilk. Stir flour and buttermilk into egg mixture, beating well. Stir in lemon rind and pecans. Pour into 2 well-greased 9-by-5-inch loaf pans and bake at 350°F. for 45–55 minutes. When done, remove loaves from pans and place on wax paper on cookie sheet. Prick holes in tops with toothpick. Combine glaze ingredients and bring to a boil on top of stove. Spoon over hot bread, covering tops completely. Cool bread thoroughly and wrap. Let stand 1–2 days before slicing.

Makes two 9-x-5-inch loaves.

MUFFINS

Hot muffins are a wonderful way to spark an otherwise unremarkable meal. Quick, easy, delicious, and endlessly variable, muffins were traditional breakfast fare on days when the week's supply of yeast bread was being made. And they were always on hand for tea and for Sunday night supper, "cook's night off."

The secret to perfect muffins is in the mixing. Blend wet and dry ingredients just enough to moisten the flour. The batter should be lumpy; if you stir enough to smooth out the lumps, you've stirred too much, and the results will be tough and uninspired. Bake at moderately high heat so the baking powder can work its best.

EVERYDAY MUFFINS

A good basic muffin recipe. Add your own touches by stirring into batter one cup berries, or by spooning one tablespoon of jam into each muffin before baking.

Sift dry ingredients together. Combine liquid ingredients and stir into dry mixture all at once, stirring just enough to moisten. Fill greased muffin tins ⅔ full and bake at 400°F. for 20–25 minutes.

Makes 12 muffins.

2   **cups flour**
2   **teaspoons baking powder**
½   **teaspoon salt**
4   **tablespoons sugar**
2   **eggs**
¾   **cup milk**
¼   **cup melted shortening**

SPICY PUMPKIN MUFFINS

Crunchy and spicy, and just the ticket to beautifully complement a roast turkey.

Sift together flour, baking powder, brown sugar, salt, and spices. In separate bowl, beat eggs and add milk and shortening to them. Stir in pumpkin and Grapenuts. Add all at once to dry ingredients, stirring only until flour is moistened. Fill greased muffin pans ⅔ full and bake at 400°F. for 20–25 minutes.

Makes 12 muffins.

2   **cups flour**
2   **teaspoons baking powder**
2   **to 4 tablespoons brown sugar**
½   **teaspoon salt**
½   **teaspoon cinnamon**
¼   **teaspoon cloves**
¼   **teaspoon ginger**
2   **eggs**
¾   **cup milk**
¼   **cup melted shortening**
½   **cup mashed, cooked pumpkin**
½   **cup Grapenuts breakfast cereal**

2 **cups flour**
2 **tablespoons sugar**
3 **teaspoons baking powder**
½ **teaspoon salt**
1 **egg**
1 **cup milk**
¼ **cup melted shortening**
¼ **cup grated American cheese**
¼ **cup chopped dates**

CHEESY DATE MUFFINS

The perfect solution when you want a hot bread that's a little bit fancy.

Sift together flour, sugar, baking powder, and salt. Beat egg and add milk and shortening to it. Add liquids to dry ingredients and stir to moisten. Fold in cheese and dates. Fill greased muffin pans ⅔ full and bake at 400°F. for 20–25 minutes.

Makes 12 muffins.

CORN BREAD AND JO(H)NNY CAKE

Actually a type of grass, corn was first taken from the jungles of the Yucatàn and Guatemala by the Mayas more than three thousand years ago. Originally no larger than a man's finger, the ear has been enlarged more than a hundredfold through selective planting and breeding over the centuries.

It was the Indians who generously imparted their knowledge about this New World staple to the English colonists, whose imported wheat and other English grains had failed to provide for that first hard winter in America. Thanks to those Indians, corn and its products became, and remain, a basic food in the New England diet. Cornmeal was made into mush (or hasty pudding), bread, fried cakes, and, of course, Indian pudding.

It is generally agreed that the name "jo(h)nny cake" probably derived from "journey cake," as cornmeal was easily transported and quickly made into cakes to be fried over an open fire, and once-fried corn cakes also were convenient to carry in the traveler's haversack for reheating at a camp site, to be served with melted butter and molasses or maple syrup.

Why the careful use of parentheses in "jo(h)nny cake"? Like so many other traditions in New England, this one is subject to happily dedicated argument, *particularly* in Rhode Island! Whereas "johnny cake" needs no parentheses in other New England states, is made of yellow cornmeal, and is eaten with molasses or maple syrup along with melted butter, in *Rhode Island*, "jonny cakes" (*no* h) are made of the special "whitecap flint" corn grown and milled exclusively in that state, and they are eaten with lashings of melted butter, but *never* with a sweet syrup. Rhode Islanders in general stand firmly behind the principle that jonny cakes are so superior to johnny cakes that little comparison is possible.

Still quoted today is "Shepherd Tom" Hazard of Narragansett (born Thomas Robinson Hazard in 1797), whose *Jonnycake Papers* state unequivocally: "The Southern epicures crack a good deal about hoecakes and hominy made from their white flint corn, the Pennsylvanians of their mush and Boston folks of their Boston brown bread, whilst one Joe Barlow, of New Haven, used to sing a long song in glorification of New England hasty pudding; but none of these reputed luxuries are worthy of holding a candle to an old-fashioned Narragansett jonny-cake made from Indian corn meal raised on the southern coast of Rhode Island."

And while we're on the subject, it should be added that corn bread is just that, a bread made of corn. Jo(h)nny cakes are small fried cakes.

JONNY CAKES

1   cup the right kind of
     jonny cake meal
     (see note below)
½   teaspoon salt
1   teaspoon sugar
1   cup boiling water
1   tablespoon butter
1   cup milk (about)

Here is one kind of Rhode Island corn cake. Breakfast, South County style.

Combine meal, salt, and sugar. Pour in boiling water, add butter, and stir to blend. Let sit 10 minutes, until meal has become swollen and soft. Stir in milk, ¼ cup at a time, until mixture is consistency of mashed potatoes. Drop by tablespoons onto hot griddle. Brown to good crust on both sides, turning once. Serve with lots of butter. (Tradition forbids use of maple syrup, but . . .)

Makes 12 cakes to serve 6.

Note: Proper jonny cake meal can be obtained by mail order, if you don't happen to be in Rhode Island, from: Ryan's Market, 70 Brown St., North Kingston, RI 02852; Gray's, Adamsville, RI 02801; Kenyon's Grist Mill, Usquepaugh, RI 02836; Dovecrest Trading Post, Exeter, RI 02822; and Prescott Farm, 2009 West Main Rd., Middletown, RI 02840. These are names and addresses current at time of publishing. Write the Rhode Island Chamber of Commerce should these addresses lapse.

FRIED INDIAN CAKES

2   cups yellow cornmeal
½   teaspoon baking soda
½   teaspoon salt
2½   cups boiling water
     (about)

Not a Rhode Island recipe! Serve with butter and maple syrup, creamed chicken, or creamed chipped beef.

Combine all ingredients to make a dough thick enough to form into thick cakes with the hands. Fry cakes in hot fat in frying pan, using enough fat to come about halfway up the sides of the cakes. Brown on one side, then turn and brown on the other. Serve hot with butter, maple syrup, and bacon.

Serves 4–6.

PIONEER CORN BREAD

A good recipe for classic corn bread or corn muffins.

Sift together dry ingredients. In small bowl, beat egg and add milk and shortening to it. Add egg mixture to dry ingredients and stir just enough to moisten. Pour into greased 8-x-8-inch pan or fill greased muffin cups ⅔ full. Bake at 400°F. for 30 minutes (bread), or for 20–25 minutes (muffins), or until edges pull away from pan or muffin cups.

Makes sixteen 2-inch squares or 12 muffins.

1 cup flour
1 cup cornmeal
1 tablespoon sugar
3 teaspoons baking powder
½ teaspoon salt
1 egg
1 cup milk
¼ cup melted shortening

DOUGHNUTS

Almost any dough has been rolled out, cut, and fried, or even boiled (though, having tried a boiled doughnut recipe, we don't recommend it) as doughnuts. Who knows where the tradition began, or where it will go from here? Every cook's imagination works its own magic, devising new shapes, new flavors, new coatings. Nothing beats a doughnut—or its hole—for breakfast, coffee-time, dessert, or snacking. Fill them, using jam or pudding of any flavor. Spice them, using a wide array of condiments to give a unique fillip. Add mashed or cut-up fruits, or change the taste and texture by combining different types of flour. They can be leavened with baking powder, baking soda, yeast, or sourdough starter, as you choose. When they're cooked, ice them, glaze them, powder or spice them, or reheat them. Then too, there's nothing better than a slightly stale doughnut, split, sprinkled with a little water if hardish, and then toasted and buttered!

Doughnuts should be deep fried in fat heated to 360–385°F.; at those temperatures the dough cooks through without either burning or absorbing too much oil.

HOMEMADE DOUGHNUTS

These rise to the top of the heap, as doughnuts go. Very light, tender, and easy to make, too.

2 eggs
1 cup sugar
2 tablespoons melted shortening
1 cup sour milk
3 to 4 cups flour
1 teaspoon salt
1 teaspoon soda
1 teaspoon nutmeg
2 tablespoons baking powder

Beat eggs and beat sugar into them. Add melted shortening and sour milk and beat well. Sift dry ingredients. Beat 2 cups of dry mixture into liquids, then beat in as much more as needed to make soft dough. Roll to ½-inch thickness, cut, and fry in deep fat heated to 385°F. Turn doughnuts as soon as they rise to surface. Serve hot, or drain and reheat briefly before eating.

Makes about 30 doughnuts.

ORANGE TEA DOUGHNUTS

Fun to make and perfect for a bake sale or church supper.

1 cup sugar
3 cups sifted flour
3 teaspoons baking powder
½ teaspoon baking soda
½ teaspoon salt
3 eggs
1 tablespoon salad oil
1 cup orange juice

Sift together dry ingredients. Beat eggs until light, and beat oil and orange juice into them. Add egg mixture to dry ingredients and stir until just moistened. Drop by tablespoonfuls into deep fat heated to 365°F. Fry until golden brown on both sides, turning once. Drain on brown paper. While still warm, sprinkle with sugar and serve.

Makes about 3 dozen.

PANCAKES

If a word association test were given on the word "pancakes," more 'n likely a large percentage of answers would be, "Maple Syrup!"

SNOW GRIDDLE CAKES

Very light and delicate, these are clearly a seasonal *treat. But treat they are. Snow is the leavener.*

6	**tablespoons flour**
¼	**teaspoon salt**
5	**tablespoons light, freshly fallen snow**
½	**cup milk**

Stir first 3 ingredients together lightly and add milk. Bake in small (2-inch) cakes on *lightly* greased, heated griddle. Spread with butter and top with maple syrup or sprinkle with sugar.

Makes 6 cakes. Serves 1.

Maple Sugaring Time

by Eden Brown

"When is maple sugaring time?" is a question often asked of me by my friends from the city and, lacking a definite answer, I usually reply, "Oh, in the springtime. About the middle of March. Depends on the weather."

And that is about it. In Vermont, springtime is sugaring time. When March comes along the signs heralding the approach of the maple sugaring season become quite obvious even though the thermometer may still go below zero occasionally and, some years, the heaviest snowfalls are yet to come. On bright, sunny days the melting snow makes little streams along the roadside and in the mornings the crows, back from the swamps and the lowlands, call across the hills, greeting each other like old friends at a convention. Town meeting day arrives and at noon the folks in the old town hall, or the new school auditorium, pause for luncheon served by the good ladies of the Grange or some other like organization. Among the menfolk the talk, sooner or later, turns to sugaring:

"Goin' to sugar this year, John?"

"Well, maybe. Need a good rain to settle the snow some. Little mite early for my place yet."

"Hear Ed James hung some yesterdee. Said it run purty good 'long in the forenoon."

"Yes, it lays to the south up there. Always did run early. Too much snow in my bush. Now, take when it melts away from the bottom of the trees, that's the time to sugar."

"I dunno, Bill. Crows are back. Ice is about to go in the river. Time to get the roads broke out and buckets scattered. Won't be long now."

And so it goes. Springtime is sugarin' time. A time of action. A time to be a part of.

—Excerpt from article originally titled
"Being a Part of Spring," in March 1960 *Yankee*

RYE PANCAKES

An interesting switch from ordinary pancakes. Serve with German or Polish sausage.

Combine ingredients and stir to blend thoroughly. Then drop by large spoonfuls onto griddle and brown on both sides. Heat mixture of 1 cup sugar and 2 tablespoons vinegar and use as syrup.

Makes 2 dozen.

3 cups rye flour
2 cups milk
1 egg
1 cup flour
1 cup sugar or molasses
1 teaspoon salt
1 teaspoon soda
2 teaspoons baking powder
1 teaspoon cream of tartar
½ cup rum

HARDSCRABBLE OATMEAL PANCAKES

Hearty fare that sticks to your ribs. Great before a morning spent chopping wood.

Combine oats and buttermilk and let stand 10 minutes. Combine dry ingredients. Add beaten egg to oats mixture, then add dry ingredients and stir until mixed. Let stand for a few minutes, then cook over low heat on lightly greased griddle. Turn cakes to brown on both sides. Top with butter and molasses sauce.

Makes 6–8 fat cakes.

¾ cup quick rolled oats
1 cup buttermilk
½ cup flour
¾ teaspoon salt
½ teaspoon baking soda
1 tablespoon sugar
1 beaten egg

Molasses Sauce

Melt butter in molasses and serve over warm cakes.

¼ cup butter
½ cup dark molasses

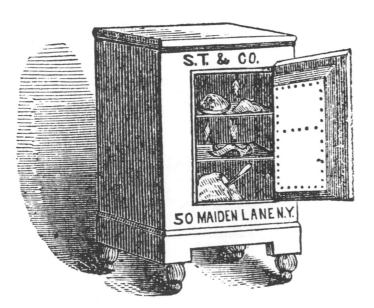

7

SALADS, DRESSINGS, AND SIDE DISHES

Salads

Herein are collected salads and dressings for every occasion: superb versions of classic chicken, lobster, potato, or shrimp salad; great green salads; decorative fruit salads, and some really great molds, aspic-ed or moussed. Salad Dressings are grouped together separately, but page references are given in salad recipes wherever a specific dressing is recommended.

APPLE RAISIN SALAD

A unique salad on the sweet side. Accompanies roast pork with style.

2 cups shredded cabbage
1 cup diced, unpared apple
1 cup seedless raisins
  Cooked Salad Dressing
    (p. 138)
  Salt and pepper

Blend cabbage, apple, and raisins. Moisten with Cooked Salad Dressing and season with salt and pepper.

Serves 6.

AVOCADO MOUSSE

Grapefruit and avocado are an unusual and unusually delicious combo. Use a silver fork to mash the avocado so as not to discolor it. Unmold on bed of torn, crisped lettuce.

Mix boiling water with lime gelatin and stir until gelatin is dissolved. Chill until of consistency of unbeaten egg whites. In another bowl, beat mashed avocado with cream cheese, mayonnaise, lemon juice, and salt until mixture is creamy. Add thickened gelatin and beat until blended. Fold sliced avocado and grapefuit sections into gelatin mixture. Rinse 1-quart mold with cold water, then pour in mousse mixture. Chill until firm.

Serves 8.

1 cup boiling water
1 package (3 ounces) lime gelatin
⅔ cup mashed avocado pulp (use 1 small avocado or ½ large)
1 package (3 ounces) cream cheese
2 tablespoons mayonnaise
2 tablespoons lemon juice
1 teaspoon salt
1 small avocado, or other half of large one, peeled, stoned, and sliced
1 cup grapefuit sections, diced and drained

CAESAR SALAD

Toasted croutons and crisp lettuce tossed with a unique and famous dressing. Make dressing first, as it must be chilled before using.

Melt butter and sauté crushed garlic in it for 3–5 minutes. Remove garlic. Add bread cubes and brown over medium heat, turning to brown on all sides. Sprinkle with Parmesan cheese. Put lettuce in salad bowl and sprinkle with browned bread croutons. Toss with Caesar Salad Dressing.

Serves 4.

2 tablespoons melted butter
1 clove garlic, skinned and crushed
1 cup fresh bread cubes (about ½ inch, remove crusts before cutting)
Parmesan cheese
1 head Boston lettuce or ½ head romaine, torn and crisped
½ cup Caesar Salad Dressing (p. 138)

CHESTNUT, GRAPE, AND CELERY SALAD

This aristocratic salad is a nice way to use up left-over chestnuts.

Chop chestnuts, add celery and grapes, and marinate in orange juice 1 hour. Drain and serve on lettuce with French Dressing.

Serves 4.

1 cup boiled or roasted chestnuts, shelled
½ cup chopped celery
1 cup blue grapes, halved and seeded
½ cup orange juice
Lettuce
French Dressing (p. 140)

"All Gone By"

by Harriette Wilbur

During a year's sojourn on a New Hampshire farm in the foothills of Mount Kearsarge, I learned that the literature concerning rural New England ignores many quaint, colorful ideas and expressions, words harking back to Chaucer and Shakespeare.

When I arrived in my car, two elderly men who had the "hay rights" were preparing to depart for the day. Both mumbled, "How be ye?" and waited. Their appraising eyes never left me.

"My lettuces be all gone by with now," explained the older farmer as I chaffered for vegetables. "Gone by with," or "gone by" never lost their droll flavor in my ears. "They be gone by with now," a small boy replied anent marsh marigold greens; once he tossed away an apple he had gathered with the disdainful comment, "It be all gone by." An aged housewife pronounced a cup custard "gone by with" and took it to the "henpen." Even a Concord tire dealer told me, "That size be pretty much gone by with nowadays."

An elderly woman, who prided herself on having been the local High School's star grammarian and valedictorian in 1876, explained, *"Gone by* dates back to when the well-to-do sent their daughters to Boston boarding-schools; they studied French and explained to the home-folks that *passé* means passed or gone by. The *with* is just trimmings, I apperhend."

—Excerpt from article originally titled
"New Hampshirisms," in July 1947 *Yankee*

CHICKEN SALAD

A delicious version of a favorite American salad.

2 **cups diced, cooked chicken**
1 **cup chopped celery**
¾ **cup mayonnaise**
¼ **cup chopped walnuts**
1 **tablespoon chopped parsley**
   Dash Tabasco sauce
   Lettuce
   Watercress or sorrel for garnish

Mix together all ingredients except lettuce and watercress or sorrel. Serve on bed of lettuce and garnish with watercress or sorrel.

Serves 6.

YANKEE COLE SLAW

A dandy cabbage salad or slaw.

Combine cabbage and celery. Mix mustard with 1 tablespoon vinegar. Heat rest of vinegar until boiling, and stir in mustard, sugar, salt and pepper, and beaten egg. Cook over low heat, stirring, until thick. Pour hot sauce over cabbage and celery and mix well. Chill and serve as is, or mix optional apple and sour cream into chilled slaw just before serving.

Serves 6.

1 **small head cabbage, shredded**
½ **bunch celery, chopped**
1 **tablespoon dry mustard**
¼ **cup vinegar**
2 **tablespoons sugar**
   Salt and pepper
1 **egg, beaten**
1 **apple, peeled, cored, and chopped (optional)**
¼ **cup sour cream (optional)**

CRANBERRY BANANA SALAD

Tart cranberry and suave banana smoothly combine in a memorable mold.

Add cold water to gelatin and let stand 2 minutes. Dissolve in boiling water. Stir into cranberry sauce. Add lemon rind and juice, banana, and nuts. Rinse a 2-cup mold, or 4 custard cups, with cold water, then pour in mixture and chill until firm. Unmold on crisp lettuce.

Serves 4.

¼ **cup cold water**
1 **envelope plain gelatin**
½ **cup boiling water**
1 **can (1 pound) whole cranberry sauce**
1 **teaspoon lemon rind**
1 **teaspoon lemon juice**
1 **banana, peeled and diced**
¼ **cup chopped walnuts**
   Lettuce

To Crisp Salad Greens

Fill sink or bowl with cold water and add greens. Swish around a bit to give any particles of dirt or sand clinging to the leaves a chance to settle to the bottom. Remove greens to a colander. Rinse again, piece by piece, removing any discolored areas or thick stems. Drain washed greens well and dry with towel. Wrap in clean towel and place in refrigerator for two hours or more before using.

FISH OR CHICKEN ASPIC

A light and refreshing luncheon salad.

2   chicken bouillon cubes
2   tablespoons plain gelatin
¼   cup cold water
1   cup boiling water
1   cup dry white wine
½   cup diced cucumber
¼   cup diced celery
2   cups cooked, flaked fish or diced, cooked chicken

Soak bouillon cubes and gelatin in cold water until soft. Add boiling water and stir until gelatin and cubes are dissolved. Stir in wine. Cool until almost set. Add cucumber, celery, and fish or chicken. Oil a 1½-quart mold and pour in aspic. Chill for several hours. Unmold on lettuce leaves and serve with a dressing of your choice.

Serves 6.

SUNDAY NIGHT SALAD BOWL

Wash all greens well, dry, wrap with clean towel, and refrigerate for an hour or two to crisp.

1   clove garlic, halved
1   bunch watercress
1   bunch chicory
1   head lettuce
3   sweet radishes, diced
3   stalks celery, chopped
1   carrot, sliced thin
3   tomatoes, cut in small chunks
1   sweet onion, chopped
3   tablespoons Roquefort cheese
3   slices bacon, cooked and crumbled
½   cup French Dressing (p. 140)

Rub a large salad bowl with garlic. Break greens into small pieces. Add other ingredients and mix thoroughly. Marinate with dressing for 30 minutes in refrigerator. Serve with additional dressing in a bowl.

Serves 4–6.

LOBSTER AND AVOCADO SALAD

A luscious lobster salad, undeniably expensive. Save a little by using frozen Rock Lobster tails (thawed, and cooked) if need be, or halve recipe. If you use Maine lobster, you'll need the meat from two steamed ones. Just don't dilute required quantity of lobster meat by substituting chicken. It simply doesn't answer!

Mix lobster with celery and sprinkle with lemon juice. Add mayonnaise and paprika. Season to taste with salt and pepper, and mix well. Fill avocado hollows with lobster mixture and garnish with watercress.

Serves 6.

2   **cups finely diced, cooked lobster meat**
½   **cup finely diced celery**
1   **teaspoon lemon juice**
½   **cup mayonnaise**
½   **teaspoon paprika**
    Salt and pepper
3   **avocados, halved and stoned**
    Watercress for garnish

NUTTY FRUIT AND VEGETABLE SALAD

Cabbage, celery, onion, carrots and walnuts tastefully combined with apples, peaches, pears, and raisins.

Combine all ingredients in salad bowl. Toss and serve with French Dressing (p. 140) or mayonnaise.

Serves 6.

1   **cup sliced, unpeeled red apples**
1   **cup peeled, sliced peaches**
1   **cup peeled, sliced pears**
1   **cup diced celery**
1   **cup diced, scraped carrots**
½   **cup raisins**
¾   **cup shredded cabbage**
¼   **cup minced onion**
½   **cup chopped walnuts**

SHRIMP SALAD

Use as suggested, or to fill stoned avocado halves.

Combine all ingredients except lettuce and eggs, and chill well. Line 4 salad plates with lettuce and divide salad evenly among them. Garnish plates with egg slices.

Serves 4.

2   **cups cleaned, cooked shrimp, or drained, canned shrimp, rinsed**
1   **teaspoon finely chopped onion**
3   **tablespoons lemon juice**
2   **cups diced celery**
⅓   **cup mayonnaise**
¼   **cup chili sauce**
    Lettuce
2   **or 3 hard-boiled eggs, sliced**

POINSETTIA SALAD

A pretty salad for any season.

8 large red apples
Lettuce
1 pint cottage cheese
1 cup crushed pineapple
1 cup nut meats
Currant Jelly Dressing
(p. 139)

Core apples and cut each into 8 sections sliced almost through to the bottom. Spread these segments apart slightly and place on bed of lettuce. Mix cottage cheese and pineapple and pile in center of each apple. Garnish with nut meats. Serve at once with Currant Jelly Dressing.

Serves 8.

It's Picnic Time

by J. Almus Russell

On turkey-red tablecloths with edges anchored down to the ground by flat granite stones, our mothers spread the picnic luncheon—and what a meal! In our section of the state [N.H.], salads were then unknown among the rural farmers. Instead we arranged plates of lettuce, peppercress, and chives (carefully removed from wet towels to insure their crispness), interspersed with white and red radishes, and balls of buttermilk cheese. A large bowl of "vinegared potato" (our homemade makeshift for the modern potato salad) flanked platters of sandwiches that *were* sandwiches (with all the glory of their crisp homemade crusts left on); chopped ham filling, red-hot with pungent English mustard; baked bean filling, rich with salt pork and spicy flavoring; sliced green-tomato pickle; and the never-failing cucumber and onion, the source of many an after-picnic case of indigestion. Some of the bolder youths bit bravely into red and green pickled peppers, taking care not to blister tender lips on treacherous rind. Others smacked them appreciatively over pickled limes and onions.

—Excerpt from July 1941 *Yankee*

POTATO SALAD

The perfect picnic fare.

Cube potatoes while hot. Mix in other ingredients except bacon and parsley. Chill. Just before serving, sprinkle with crumbled bacon and chopped parsley.

Serves 6.

6 medium potatoes, peeled, boiled, and drained
¼ cup chopped onion
½ cup chopped celery
¾ cup mayonnaise
1½ teaspoons prepared mustard
Salt and pepper to taste
4 slices crisp, cooked bacon, crumbled
1 tablespoon chopped parsley

TOMATO ASPIC

3 cups unseasoned tomato
   juice
1½ medium onions, peeled
   and grated
4 small stalks celery,
   minced
1 medium carrot, scraped
   and minced
1 bay leaf
½ teaspoon sugar
2 tablespoons (2 envelopes)
   plain gelatin
½ cup water
2 tablespoons lemon juice
¼ teaspoon Worcestershire
   sauce
½ teaspoon salt
   Pinch pepper

Decorative, nourishing, and decidedly tasty way to set off or accompany a whole slew of different salads. The vegetables lend a crisp and tangy crunch.

Put tomato juice in saucepan with onions, celery, carrot, bay leaf, and sugar. Bring to boil, turn down heat, and simmer until celery and carrots are tender-crisp (about 15 minutes). Remove bay leaf. Put gelatin in small bowl, and add water. Let soak about 6–8 minutes. Stir gelatin into tomato mixture and add lemon juice, Worcestershire sauce, salt, and pepper. Stir well. Rinse a 3-cup mold with cold water and pour in aspic mixture. Refrigerate overnight or until well set. When ready to serve, immerse mold for a second or two in pan of hot water. Place serving platter on top of mold, and invert. With large metal mixing spoon, strike top and sides of mold sharply a few times. Then remove mold. If you used a ring mold, fill ring with salad, and garnish outside of ring with lettuce. If you used a solid mold, surround aspic with salad, and garnish likewise with lettuce.

Serves 8, with salad.

SUPER SPINACH SALAD

1 package (10 ounces) fresh
   spinach
1 small head Boston or
   Buttercrunch lettuce
⅛ teaspoon garlic powder
   Salt and pepper
½ cup thinly sliced water
   chestnuts
4 hard-boiled eggs,
   quartered
2 teaspoons drained capers
2 avocados, peeled, stoned,
   and sliced
1 cup diced cheddar cheese
1 can (4½ ounces) shrimp,
   rinsed and drained
2 large tomatoes, sliced
   vertically
   Salad dressing

Preceded by jellied consommé and accompanied by fresh, crusty French bread, a super summer meal indeed!

Wash spinach and lettuce, and tear up into largish pieces, after removing tough stems from spinach leaves. Crisp in refrigerator. Then put alternate layers of lettuce and spinach in large salad bowl, and sprinkle with garlic powder, and salt and pepper. Top with remaining ingredients except dressing and toss well. Add 1 cup dressing (Caesar Salad Dressing, p. 138, or French Dressing, p. 138, or Spicy Salad Dressing, p. 138), and toss again. Serve, passing additional salad dressing.

Serves 6–8.

TUNA MACARONI SALAD

Serve in the center of a tomato aspic ring (see opposite page) on a bed of crisp lettuce.

Mix all together and serve as above.

Serves 8.

1 cup drained and flaked white tuna-fish
½ envelope dry onion soup mix
2 tablespoons parsley
1 tablespoon chives
¼ cup pitted ripe olives
1 cup cooked macaroni
½ cup mayonnaise
½ cup sour cream
½ cup chopped celery

Salad Dressings

Sallets were originally raw vegetables dressed with salt, from which derived the name "sallet" that eventually evolved into our "salad." Here is a recipe for an "oxoleon," or dressing, from *Evylyn's Acetaria*, a 240-page discourse on sallets published in London, 1699. (Mr. Evylyn considered that there were "seventy-five herbs proper and fit to make Sallet with.")

"Take of clear and perfectly good *Oyl-Olive* three parts—of sharpest *Vinegar* (*sweetest* of all *Condiments*, for it incites appetite, and causes Hunger, which is the best sauce), *Limon*, or juice of *Orange*, one part—and therein let steep some slices of *Horseradish*, with a little *Salt:* some, in a separate Vinegar, gently bruise a pod of *Ginny* Pepper, and strain it to the other—then add as much *Mustard*, as will lie upon a half-crown piece. Beat and mingle these well together with the yolk of two new-laid *Eggs* boiled hard, and pour it over your Sallet, stirring it well together. The *super*-curious insist that the knife with which Sallet herb is cut must be of Silver—and some who are husbands of their Oyl pour at first the Oyl alone, as more apt to communicate and diffuse its slipperiness, than when it is mingled and beaten with the Acids—which they pour on last of all; and it is incredible how small a quantity of Oyl thus applied is sufficient to imbue a very plentiful asembly of Sallet Herbs."

CAESAR SALAD DRESSING

1   egg, in shell
¾   cup salad oil
2   tablespoons lemon juice
½   teaspoon salt
¼   teaspoon pepper
½   teaspoon Worcestershire
     sauce
¼   cup grated Parmesan
     cheese

Easy to make, but almost impossible to buy as a commercial bottled dressing. Good on fish or baked potato as well as on many salads other than Caesar Salad.

Drop egg into boiling water and leave for exactly 1 minute. Take egg out, break into small bowl, and beat until light and lemon colored. Add oil gradually, continuing to beat. Beat in lemon juice, seasonings, and cheese. Refrigerate in covered jar (should be used well chilled).

Makes about 1⅓ cups.

COOKED SALAD DRESSING

1   teaspoon salt
1   teaspoon dry mustard
     Dash cayenne
2   tablespoons flour
2   tablespoons sugar
2   egg yolks or 1 whole egg,
     beaten
1   cup evaporated milk
4   tablespoons lemon juice

Looks like mayonnaise, though thicker and less oily, and has a flavor all its own. Good dressing for any cabbage slaw.

Blend salt, mustard, cayenne, flour, and sugar. Add beaten egg yolks or whole egg. Mix well, then add milk. Cook in double boiler over boiling water, stirring as needed, until mixture thickens. Cool, then stir in lemon juice slowly.

Makes 1⅓ cups.

SPICY SALAD DRESSING

1   cup salad oil
⅛   cup wine vinegar
½   teaspoon garlic powder
     or garlic salt
1   teaspoon ginger
1   teaspoon nutmeg
1   bottle (8 ounces) catsup
1   teaspoon lemon juice
1   teaspoon curry powder
1   teaspoon cinnamon
½   teaspoon salt
½   teaspoon coarse black
     pepper

A dressing with real dash that will keep indefinitely if refrigerated. Serve with green salad (a "natural" for raw spinach, too).

Combine all ingredients and shake vigorously in pint jar. Refrigerate.

Makes 2 cups.

Flavored Vinegars

A wonderful adjunct to the kitchen cabinet, and a welcome gift, flavored vinegars couldn't be easier to make. Get together the bottles and jars you collect just because it seems a shame to throw away perfectly good glass, capped jars. Wash the caps and jars, put into a large pot with water to cover, and bring to a boil. Boil for 20 minutes. Drain jars and caps and add vinegar and flavorings as shown in the chart below. Each combination of vinegar and flavoring will make 1 pint of flavored vinegar. (If garlic is used, it must be removed from the vinegar after 24 hours.) Cap well and store for at least 2 weeks. Then strain and rebottle in glass bottles sterilized as before. Label.

VINEGAR (2 cups)	FLAVORING
Apple cider	2 teaspoons grated horseradish root, dash Tabasco sauce, and ¼ teaspoon black pepper
Apple cider, white, or white wine	2 large sprigs of any one of the following fresh herbs. dill, marjoram, mint, rosemary, sage, tarragon, or thyme
Apple cider, white, white wine, or red wine	¼ cup sliced onion, and pinch nutmeg
White or white wine	4 small, whole red chili peppers, or ¾ cup fresh rose petals
White wine or red wine	2 crushed cloves garlic and 1 large sprig marjoram or thyme
Red wine	1 tablespoon mace, 3 peppercorns, 4 whole cloves, 5 whole allspice, and 1 cinnamon stick

CURRANT JELLY DRESSING

A sweet-sour dressing for fruit salads.

In small bowl set in cracked ice, place dry ingredients and vinegar. Slowly add oil, beating with each addition. Beat in jelly, one spoonful at a time.

Makes about ½ cup.

¼ teaspoon mustard
¼ teaspoon salt
⅛ teaspoon black pepper
½ teaspoon powdered sugar
  Dash cayenne
2 tablespoons vinegar
4 tablespoons olive oil
2 heaping tablespoons currant jelly

FRENCH DRESSING

½ teaspoon salt
¼ teaspoon pepper
¼ teaspoon sugar
½ teaspoon dry mustard
¼ cup lime juice
   (or lemon juice, or
   vinegar)
¾ cup salad oil
   (olive, corn, or
   vegetable)
1 clove garlic, peeled

Everyone has a favorite combination of the basic ingredients for this ubiquitous and all-purpose dressing. This is Yankee's. (*We note that tomato soup is not an ingredient of* real *French Dressing, which is* not *orange!*) *Use immediately or within two or three days.*

Combine salt, pepper, sugar, and dry mustard. Add lime juice gradually until seasonings are dissolved. Pour into 8-ounce glass jar with tight cap. Add oil, ¼ cup at a time, cover jar, and shake vigorously after each addition. Drop garlic clove into jar, cap, and refrigerate. If dressing is to be refrigerated more than 1 day, remove garlic clove after 24 hours.

Makes about 1 cup.

Side Dishes

Whereas many salads are full meals in themselves, a side dish is not intended to be anything but a sidelight, which, properly chosen to complement the main course, can contribute a great deal to the overall taste and appearance of a meal. Here is an assortment.

CHESTNUT PUREE

Served as a side dish with the roast turkey for Thanksgiving or Christmas, this is a holiday tradition that is well worth the effort involved. Save time by asking other members of the family to cut the chestnuts before cooking.

1 pound chestnuts in the
   shell
1 beef bouillon cube
   Water to cover
2 tablespoons butter
¼ cup heavy cream
   Pinch black pepper
½ teaspoon sherry
1 tablespoon beef bouillon

With a sharp knife, cut a cross through the shell and skin on the round side of each chestnut. Put cut chestnuts into saucepan with bouillon cube. Add water to cover and bring to a boil. Turn down heat and simmer for about 40 minutes, or until shells loosen, cuts open up, and nut meats are tender. Turn off heat, but leave in boiling water. With slotted spoon, dip out a few chestnuts at a time, and shell, taking care to remove the thin, tough brown skin as well. Discard any moldy (greenish) or rotten (black) nut meats. If shells get harder to remove as you get near the end of the nuts to be shelled, reheat briefly. Put nut meats through a ricer or food grinder twice; or, if you are lucky enough to have an electric food processor, puree them. (A blender is not usually strong enough for the job, but by adding the other ingredients while blending—the nuts alone are too dry for the blender to work properly—you *can* manage.) You should have about 2 cups pureed chestnuts. Place pureed nuts in top of double boiler over boiling water. Beat in remaining ingredients. Either serve immediately, or refrigerate and reheat when needed in double boiler over hot water. Or freeze, defrost, and heat in double boiler as required.

Serves 6–8.

Picking Potatoes

by Mel Allen

There's no easy way to pick potatoes. There never was and there never will be. You bend over, put the basket between your legs, and move forward, picking with both hands. As long as you keep moving you won't stiffen up. Your legs go first, then your back. But more painful than either is when your wrists begin to swell. For a few days you feel terrible. Then you get used to it and concentrate on filling barrels at 40 cents a barrel.

—Excerpt from article originally titled "There's No Easy Way to Pick Potatoes," in September 1978 *Yankee*

NEW POTATOES WITH MUSTARD BUTTER

2   pounds new potatoes
6   tablespoons melted butter
1   teaspoon prepared
    mustard
1   tablespoon chopped
    parsley

There is nothing better than new potatoes with butter. Here is a version that gives this famous dish a new bite.

Wash potatoes, and peel if desired. Cook until tender in salted water. Drain. Mix butter with mustard and parsley. Pour over potatoes.

Serves 4–6.

HASTY PUDDING

1   cup yellow cornmeal
1   teaspoon salt
1   cup cold water
3   cups boiling water

Also known as cornmeal mush (or pup flup!). Eat hot with cream and sugar or butter and syrup; or chill, slice, brown slices in butter, and serve with melted butter and maple syrup.

Mix cornmeal and salt with cold water. Pour slowly into boiling water, stirring constantly to prevent lumping. Return to boil, still stirring. Reduce heat, cover pan, and let simmer over low heat (or over hot water in double boiler) for 5–10 minutes, stirring from time to time.

Serves 6.

POTATOES DELMONICO

Diced, cooked potatoes and hard-boiled eggs in a chive-y, cheesy cream sauce. Use any cheese, from a sharp cheddar to a mild Gruyère.

4	tablespoons butter
4	tablespoons flour
2	cups milk
½	teaspoon salt
¼	teaspoon pepper
½	cup diced or coarsely grated cheese
1	tablespoon snipped chives
2½	cups peeled, diced, cooked potatoes
8	hard-boiled eggs, sliced Paprika

Melt butter, blend in flour, cook a minute or so, stirring, and gradually add milk, stirring as needed. Cook until all milk has been added and sauce has thickened. Season with salt and pepper, and add cheese. Continue to cook over medium heat until cheese has melted. Stir in chives. In greased 2-quart casserole dish, place layer of potatoes, top with layer of egg slices, and cover with half the cheese sauce. Repeat, ending with sauce. Sprinkle with paprika and bake at 400°F. until bubbling.

Serves 6.

MASHED POTATOES AND CHESTNUTS

A marvelous combination!

1	pound chestnuts
3	medium potatoes
	Salt and pepper to taste
2	tablespoons butter
1	cup milk or cream

Prepare chestnuts as described for Chestnut Puree (see p. 141). Peel potatoes and cut up. Steam or boil until tender. Drain potatoes and mash. Stir in chestnuts, seasonings, butter, and milk or cream, and beat in bowl over hot water until mixture becomes fluffy.

Serves 6–8.

DUCHESS POTATOES

Bake as flat cakes brushed with beaten egg on buttered baking sheet at 400°F. until browned, or pipe through pastry tube to form decorative border around the edges of planks or baking dishes.

2	cups hot mashed or riced potatoes
2	tablespoons butter
½	teaspoon salt
2	egg yolks, lightly beaten
½	teaspoon grated Parmesan cheese
	Cream (optional)

Beat all ingredients except optional cream together until well blended. If potatoes are to be used as a border, add cream as necessary to achieve a consistency proper for the pastry tube.

Serves 4.

Maine Tea

(And "An Admirable Substitute for Mashed Potatoes")

by Tom Duke

The other day I read in the papers where a fellow said that he didn't believe that Maine men could be as rock-ribbed and tough-thewed as they are cracked up to be because he had heard that the favorite beverage of State-of-Mainers is tea. And, he asked, whoever heard of a strong man drinking tea?

Now that he has brought the matter up, and to ward off any future misconceptions, it might be a good idea to go into it thoroughly.

It is true that among real State-of-Mainers tea is considered to be the drink par excellence. But—and this is an important "but"—it is tea that is prepared in the Maine manner.

We will admit that tea prepared in the ordinary way is so weak and helpless that often it has to be carried to the table on a stretcher. Maine tea, however, is something else again. It is a virile brew that, as you shall see, has more than its share of authority. As a matter of cold fact, laboratory tests have proved that tea prepared in the Maine fashion is far more corrosive than nitric acid and only misses being the universal solvent by an eyelash.

To be at its best, Maine tea should be prepared out-of-doors in a pot made of double thick armor plate. A pound of tea to a tablespoon of water is the ratio generally observed in mixing the ingredients. This mixture is boiled for two days or until the foliage within a radius of three miles has been withered by the strong fumes it gives off. Another way of telling if the brew is ready for consumption is to drop a few old axes in the pot. When the axes are softened to a point where they can be readily mashed with a fork it can be assumed that the tea is ready to drink. The mashed axes, by the way, are not thrown away but are saved and relished as an admirable substitute for mashed potatoes.

—Excerpt from March 1940 *Yankee*

GLAZED PEARS

A fine side-dish for any roast. Also good served warm with cream as dessert.

Dip pears in melted butter and arrange in shallow baking pan. Sprinkle other ingredients over them. Broil or bake at 450°F. until browned.

Serves 4.

8   **halves canned pears, drained**
4   **tablespoons butter, melted**
½   **cup maple or dark brown sugar**
¼   **teaspoon cinnamon**
⅛   **teaspoon cloves (¼ teaspoon if using as a garnish)**
1   **tablespoon lemon juice**
⅛   **teaspoon salt**

MANDARIN RICE

Perfect complement to Spiced Roast Duck (p. 39).

Sauté celery and onion in butter until vegetables are limp. Stir in remaining ingredients. Spoon into greased 1½-quart casserole, cover, and bake in oven with duck.

Serves 8–10.

3   **tablespoons finely chopped celery**
3   **tablespoons finely chopped onion**
2   **tablespoons butter**
2   **cups bread cubes**
1   **teaspoon salt**
   Pepper
2   **cans (11 ounces each) Mandarin oranges, drained, or 4 oranges, peeled, sectioned, and cleaned of all white membrane**
1   **teaspoon poultry seasoning**
1½   **cups cooked rice, or 2 cups mashed potatoes**
1   **cup chicken broth**

LEMON APPLES

A flattering accompaniment to roast goose, baked ham, or pork.

8   **medium apples, peeled and cored**
2   **tablespoons butter**
    Brown sugar
1   **teaspoon grated lemon peel**
½   **cup water**
½   **cup white wine**
1   **tablespoon lemon juice**

Cut apples into thick slices and sauté them in butter until lightly colored. Sprinkle with brown sugar and lemon peel and pour in water, wine, and lemon juice. Cover and simmer slowly for 15–20 minutes, until apples are tender.

Serves 6–8.

8

CAKES AND COOKIES

Cakes

SOME GOOD ADVICE

Dry ingredients. Dampness in dry ingredients or in the weather will produce heaviness in cake. Keep all items in tightly sealed containers, and do not bake when the weather is humid.

Mix warm. During cold weather, warm all ingredients to a uniform temperature; they will mix together better.

Sugar. If sugar is lumpy, crumble it, and sift before adding.

Beating eggs. During cold weather, raw eggs will beat faster if they are placed, in the shell, in warm water for a short time before being broken.

Separating eggs. The quickest way to separate an egg yolk from a white is to carefully break the egg into a plate and then lift out the yolk with the fingers, allowing the white to fall between them.

Mixing bowls. Always use an earthenware bowl or pan for mixing cake. In cold weather, pour hot water into the mixing bowl to warm it, then wipe it dry. This facilitates the blending of butter and sugar.

Beating and stirring. A good cook must know the difference between beating and stirring. Stirring merely mixes the different ingredients together, while beating carries in air and thoroughly distributes it through the mass. In baking, this air expands and makes the cake light.

BLUEBERRY CAKE

¾ cup sugar
2 eggs, separated
3 cups flour
1 tablespoon baking
      powder
½ teaspoon salt
2 tablespoons melted
      butter
1½ cups milk
1 to 1½ cups blueberries,
      dusted with flour

A smooth, finely textured cake that can also be made in a bundt pan.

Beat together sugar and egg yolks. Sift together flour, baking powder, and salt, and add to eggs and sugar alternately with mixed butter and milk. Beat egg whites until stiff and gently fold into mixture, along with blueberries. (Do not overmix.) Bake in greased and floured 9-inch-square pan at 400°F. for 30 minutes.

Makes one 9-x-9-inch cake.

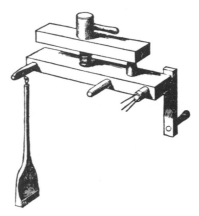

YANKEE APPLE CAKE

2 cups flour
4 teaspoons baking powder
½ teaspoon salt
2 tablespoons butter
1 egg
1 cup plus 2 tablespoons
      milk
4 large or 6 medium apples,
      peeled, cored, and
      thinly sliced
2 tablespoons sugar
½ teaspoon cinnamon

Use tart apples with lots of flavor.

Sift together flour, baking powder, and salt. Cut butter into mixture. Add egg and milk and mix well. Pour dough into greased 8-inch-square pan and cover top with neat rows of apple slices. Mix together sugar and cinnamon and sprinkle over apples. Bake at 400°F. for 25–30 minutes. Serve hot with Lemon Sauce (see below).

Makes one 8-x-8-inch cake.

Lemon Sauce

1 cup sugar
2 tablespoons cornstarch
¼ teaspoon salt
2 cups boiling water
      Grated rind and
      juice of 1 lemon
1 tablespoon butter

In saucepan mix together sugar, cornstarch, and salt. Gradually stir in hot water. Bring to boil, reduce heat, and cook until sauce is thick and clear, stirring constantly. Remove from heat and stir in lemon rind, juice, and butter. Serve hot.

Makes 2½ cups.

BOSTON CREAM PIE

You don't have to be from Boston to like this light, custard-filled, chocolate-frosted dessert cake. Use the batter to make Washington Pie, too. For Washington Pie, bake as below, fill layers with raspberry jam, and sprinkle top with confectioners' sugar.

Cake

Sift together flour, baking powder, and salt. Cream together butter and sugar until light. Beat in eggs. Gradually add flour mixture alternately with milk, beating until smooth. Add vanilla. Bake in 2 greased 9-inch layer pans at 375°F. for 25 minutes. Cool. Spread cooled Custard Filling (see below) between layers. Spread Chocolate Glaze (see further below) over top of cake.

Makes one 9-inch layer cake.

2	cups flour
2	teaspoons baking powder
½	teaspoon salt
4	tablespoons butter
1	cup sugar
2	eggs
¾	cup milk
1	teaspoon vanilla

Custard Filling

Combine flour, sugar, and salt. Add milk and egg yolks. Cook in double boiler over boiling water, stirring constantly until thickened—about 5 minutes. Cool. Stir in vanilla.

2	tablespoons flour
½	cup sugar
¼	teaspoon salt
1	cup milk
2	egg yolks, beaten
½	teaspoon vanilla

Chocolate Glaze

Mix ingredients together and spread on top of pie.

1	cup confectioners' sugar
6	tablespoons cocoa
3	tablespoons butter
1	teaspoon vanilla
6	to 8 tablespoons hot water

Nothing but Herself

by Horace Reynolds

Wedding customs are many and persistent. Everyone knows the old rhyme which declares that a bride should wear

Something old and something new,
Something borrowed and something blue.

And the wedding party still hurls rice and shoes after the bride and groom even if with little knowledge of what the act means. But there is one curious wedding custom, particularly associated with New England, which, so far as I know, has survived only in anecdote. This is the custom of the smock marriage.

One of these smock marriages is recorded in Hall's *History of Eastern Vermont.* When Asa Averill of Westminster, Vermont, married his second wife, the widow of Major Peter Lovejoy, he did so in a quite peculiar fashion. By the side of the chimney in the widow's house was a recess of some size. Across the mouth of this a blanket was stretched so as to form a closet of sorts. Into this went Mrs. Lovejoy, who disrobed and threw her clothes back into the room. Thrusting her hand through a small opening made in the blanket, Mrs. Lovejoy found the hand of Mr. Averill, clasped it, and was so married to him. He then passed her wedding attire into the recess. Putting this on, the new Mrs. Averill came out of the recess to receive the congratulations of the company.

A notice of another Vermont marriage of this sort appears in W. C. Prime's pleasant little book about New England. "In 1789," writes Mr. Prime, "at the old Field mansion on the 22d of February, Major Moses Joy was married to Mrs. Hannah Ward, widow of William Ward. This William Ward had died insolvent, leaving debts of considerable amount. At the second marriage Mrs. Ward stood in a closet with no clothing on, and held out her hand to Major Joy through a hole, and the ceremony was thus performed."

Both instances are examples of what is variously called smock marriage, shift marriage, or *mariage en chemise.* These marriages took place in the belief that if the husband takes a wife with nothing on (or just a simple smock or shift), he avoids any responsibility for her debts or the debts of her former husband. It was an English custom imported into New England and some of the other states.

—Excerpt from article in February 1965 *Yankee*

BRIDE'S CAKE

A fine cake for any special occasion. Plenty to serve twenty.

Sift together flour, baking powder, and salt. Cream butter and sugar until fluffy. Beat egg yolks until light and add to creamed mixture along with milk, vanilla, citron, raisins, and almonds. Add flour ½ cup at a time, beating well after each addition. Beat egg whites until stiff and fold into batter. Grease 10-inch tube pan, line it with waxed paper, and grease paper. Bake at 275°F. for 2 hours. Remove from oven, unmold, and frost with White Frosting (see below).

Makes one large cake.

3	cups flour
1½	teaspoons baking powder
¼	teaspoon salt
1¾	cups butter
2	cups sugar
8	eggs, separated
2	tablespoons milk
1	teaspoon vanilla
1	cup chopped citron
1	cup chopped raisins
1	cup chopped almonds

White Frosting

Cream butter and sugar. Beat in vanilla, salt, and cream until frosting is of spreading consistency.

Makes about 1 cup.

¼	cup butter
2	cups confectioners' sugar
1	teaspoon vanilla
¼	teaspoon salt
3	tablespoons heavy cream

ELECTION CAKE

Like the Italian panettone *and Russian* koulitch, *this is somewhere between a bread and a cake—rather like a rich and fruited Danish pastry. Election cake was traditionally made for Election Day and either served at the church supper preceding town meeting, or sold outside the polling place—like a one-cake bake sale—to help sustain the voters.*

1	cup scalded milk
¼	cup brown sugar
¼	teaspoon salt
1	package dry yeast
1	cup flour
¾	cup white sugar
⅓	cup butter
2	eggs, beaten
1½	cups boiling water
¾	cup white raisins
¼	cup diced citron or diced dried apricots
¼	teaspoon nutmeg
¼	teaspoon mace
¼	cup flour
3	cups flour

Combine milk with brown sugar and salt. Cool to lukewarm. Sprinkle yeast over milk and stir until dissolved. Gradually stir in 1 cup flour. Let this sponge mixture rise in warm place until doubled and fluffy, about 1 hour. Cream white sugar and butter and beat in eggs. Pour boiling water over raisins in a pan and let stand about 20 minutes, or until raisins are plumped. Drain. Add citron or apricots, spices, and ¼ cup flour to raisins and mix. Stir raisins into creamed mixture and mix well. Add to sponge. Stir in 3 cups flour little by little until dough becomes kneadable. Then knead in last of flour and continue to knead dough in bowl until smooth and satiny. Divide dough in half, and place each half in greased and floured 8-x-4-inch loaf pan. Cover pans with foil or towel and place in refrigerator to rise overnight. In the morning, bake at 375°F. for 30 minutes. Remove from pans and cool on rack. When almost cool, spread tops with Confectioners' Sugar Glaze.

Makes two 8-x-4-inch loaves.

Confectioners' Sugar Glaze

Combine ingredients, blending until smooth.

¾ cup sifted confectioners' sugar
1 to 2 tablespoons milk
Dash vanilla

CRANBERRY PUDDING CAKE

A nice, moist, yellow cake studded with cranberries and served with sauce; typical of desserts popular at the turn of the century. A pretty dessert cake. Egg Sauce is also known as Foamy Sauce.

Cream butter and sugar. Sift together flour, baking powder, and salt. Beat egg, vanilla, and water into creamed mixture alternately with flour. Stir in cranberries. Pour into greased 8-inch-square pan and bake in 350°F. oven for 30–35 minutes. Cut into 2-inch squares and serve with Egg Sauce (see below).

Makes sixteen 2-inch squares.

¼ cup melted butter
1 cup sugar
1½ cups flour
2 teaspoons baking powder
½ teaspoon salt
1 egg
1 teaspoon vanilla
½ cup cold water
1 cup cranberries

Egg Sauce

In top of double boiler cream together butter and sugar. Place over simmering water, beat in eggs and salt, and continue beating until smooth, about 5 minutes. Flavor with vanilla and serve immediately.

Makes 1½ cups.

½ cup butter
1 cup confectioners' sugar
2 eggs
¼ teaspoon salt
1 teaspoon vanilla (or rum, sherry, or brandy)

SALT PORK CAKE

1 cup hot coffee
½ pound salt pork, rind removed, finely chopped in blender or meat grinder
½ cup molasses
½ cup sugar
1 egg, beaten
2 teaspoons baking soda
2 cups flour
1½ teaspoons powdered cloves
1½ teaspoons powdered allspice
½ pound raisins
½ pound currants

In the winter, when the cow went dry, and the lard in the larder was almost gone, New England ingenuity turned to salt pork as a shortening. Soak salt pork in water overnight to remove some of the salt before chopping. This is a dense and moist gingerbread cake.

Pour coffee over salt pork and stir in molasses, sugar, and egg. Sift together baking soda, flour, cloves, and allspice, and blend into molasses mixture. Stir in raisins and currants and beat well. Grease and flour a 9-inch-square pan. Pour in batter and bake at 350°F. for 1 hour.

Makes one 9-inch cake.

ORANGE ALMOND CAKE

½ cup butter
½ cup sugar
½ cup honey
1 tablespoon grated orange rind
5 egg yolks
1¾ cups flour
2 teaspoons baking powder
½ teaspoon salt
½ cup orange juice

Just fantastic!

Cream butter and sugar. Add honey and orange rind and mix well. Beat in egg yolks one at a time. Sift together dry ingredients and add to creamed mixture alternately with orange juice. Beat all together, then turn into greased and floured 9-x-13-inch pan and bake at 350°F. for 50–55 minutes. Cool on rack. When cool, frost with Toasted Almond Icing (see below). Cut into 1-x-2-inch bars.

Makes 58 bars.

Toasted Almond Icing

3 tablespoons butter
3 tablespoons heavy cream
Confectioners' sugar
½ teaspoon orange juice
Dash lemon juice
½ teaspoon grated orange rind
¼ cup finely chopped almonds, lightly toasted

Cream butter with heavy cream and confectioners' sugar, beating well and adding enough sugar to make icing of spreadable consistency. Beat in juices and orange rind. Ice cake, and sprinkle with toasted chopped almonds.

MUSTER GINGERBREAD

This makes up into a thin slab of the spicy hard gingerbread that used to be sold in squares for a few pennies each on "Muster Days" to spectators who turned out to watch the local militia drill. Today in New England, a "muster" refers to a competition between teams of firemen with old-fashioned hand-powered "pumpers," the winning team being the one either to be in action first, from a designated starting point, or to send the stream of water from its pumper the farthest distance. Like European "card" gingerbread, this can be baked in flat molds, to come out, for example, as a 10- to 12-inch soldier.

⅓	cup butter
⅓	cup brown sugar
1	egg, well beaten
½	cup molasses
2	cups sifted flour
1½	teaspoons ginger
½	teaspoon cinnamon
¾	teaspoon salt
½	teaspoon baking powder
1	tablespoon white sugar
1	teaspoon instant coffee

Cream butter and brown sugar until fluffy. Stir in egg and molasses. Sift together flour, spices, salt, and baking powder. Add to creamed mixture, and stir until smooth. Chill thoroughly. Roll dough ¼ inch thick on lightly floured board and place on greased cookie sheet or flat mold. Combine white sugar and instant coffee and sprinkle over top of gingerbread in cookie sheet. Bake for 20 minutes at 350°F. Remove from oven and cut into squares. *Or*, unmold, and then sprinkle with the white sugar and instant coffee. Put under broiler just enough to melt topping.

Makes 1 dozen squares.

POUND CAKE

1 cup shortening
2 cups sugar
2 eggs
¼ teaspoon salt
2 teaspoons baking soda
2 cups buttermilk
4½ cups flour
¾ cup dried currants
1 teaspoon flour

This cake originally got its name because it required a pound each of butter, sugar, and flour. A dozen eggs were added to make it rise; it contained no baking powder. This newer version of the recipe is much easier to make.

Cream together shortening and sugar until fluffy. Add eggs one at a time and beat until smooth. Add salt. Stir baking soda into buttermilk and mix rapidly until bubbles form. Then add buttermilk alternately with flour to creamed mixture, beating well after each addition. Combine currants with 1 teaspoon flour and stir lightly into batter. Pour into greased 9-x-5-inch loaf pan and bake at 350°F. for 50–60 minutes. Turn out onto rack and cool.

Makes one 9-x-5-inch loaf.

POPPY SEED CAKE

1 cup scalded milk
1 cup poppy seeds, broken up in blender or coffee grinder
1 teaspoon vanilla
½ cup butter
2 cups sugar
2½ cups flour
½ teaspoon salt
1 tablespoon baking powder
5 egg whites

Make this cake with very thin layers.

Pour milk over poppy seeds and let cool. Stir in vanilla. Cream butter and sugar. Sift together flour, salt, and baking powder. Add poppy seed mixture to creamed mixture alternately with dry ingredients. Beat egg whites until stiff and fold into batter. Divide among 3 greased and floured 9-inch cake pans and bake at 350°F. for 20 minutes. When cool, fill with Chocolate Cream Filling (see below), and frost with Chocolate Butter Cream Frosting (p. 158).

Makes one 9-inch layer cake.

Chocolate Cream Filling

2 cups milk
1 square baking chocolate
2 eggs, beaten
¾ cup sugar
4 tablespoons flour
¼ teaspoon salt
2 tablespoons butter
1 teaspoon vanilla

Combine milk with chocolate in double boiler top and scald. Mix eggs, sugar, flour, and salt and combine with milk. Heat 10 minutes over boiling water, stirring constantly. Do not let mixture reach a boil. Stir in butter. Cool and add vanilla.

Makes about 2½ cups.

FRUIT CAKE

Fruit cakes were often steamed in New England, and thus made like brown bread. Later recipes call for them to be first steamed, and then baked. This one is cooked in the oven only. It will keep for months in the refrigerator.

4	cups flour
½	teaspoon baking soda
1	teaspoon mace
1	teaspoon cinnamon
½	teaspoon ginger
2	pounds currants
2	pounds raisins
½	pound chopped citron
2	cups sliced almonds or walnuts
1	pound butter
2	cups brown sugar
8	eggs, separated
½	cup brandy

Sift together flour, soda, and spices. Toss in fruit and nuts. Cream together butter and brown sugar until fluffy and beat in egg yolks. Add flour and fruit to creamed mixture alternately with brandy. Fold in stiffly beaten egg whites. Pour into 2 greased 9-x-5-inch loaf pans lined with waxed paper. Bake at 275°F. for 3 hours.

Makes two 9-x-5-inch loaf cakes.

VERMONT CHOCOLATE POTATO CAKE

2½   cups sifted flour
4   teaspoons baking powder
½   teaspoon salt
½   teaspoon cinnamon
½   teaspoon cloves
¼   teaspoon nutmeg
¼   teaspoon allspice
¾   cup butter
2   cups sugar
3   squares unsweetened chocolate, melted
1   cup freshly mashed potato
2   eggs, separated
½   teaspoon vanilla
½   teaspoon almond extract
¾   cup milk
1   cup chopped nuts

½   cup butter
3   cups confectioners' sugar
½   cup cocoa
¼   cup cream
1   teaspoon vanilla

A moist, rich cake, good frosted, or simply dusted with confectioners' sugar.

Sift together flour, baking powder, salt, and spices. Cream butter until soft, add sugar, and beat until fluffy. Add melted chocolate and potato, and beat until smooth. Beat egg yolks and add with vanilla and almond extract. Add flour alternately with milk and blend in nuts. Beat egg whites until stiff and fold in. Bake in greased 10-inch tube pan at 350°F. for 1 hour. Cool, turn onto rack, and frost with Chocolate Butter Cream Frosting (see below).

Makes one large cake.

Chocolate Butter Cream Frosting

Cream together butter, sugar, and cocoa. Blend in cream and vanilla and beat until smooth. Makes about 3 cups—enough to frost sides and top of Vermont Chocolate Potato Cake or Poppy Seed Cake (p. 156).

GREAT GRANDMOTHER'S SPONGE CAKE

2   cups sugar
4   eggs
2   cups flour
2   teaspoons baking powder
2   teaspoons vanilla
¼   teaspoon salt
1   cup hot milk
4   tablespoons melted butter

This age-hallowed recipe is very nearly foolproof. Works even for people who have "tried for years to make a sponge cake, without success." Serve with your favorite frosting, or topped with sweetened fresh berries.

In large bowl beat together 1 cup sugar and 2 eggs until fluffy. Add remaining sugar and eggs, beating constantly. Sift together flour and baking powder 3 times and gradually add to mixture. Add vanilla and salt. Stir in hot milk and melted butter. Pour into greased and floured 10-inch tube pan. Bake at 350°F. for 40–45 minutes. Cool on rack.

Makes 1 cake.

STRAWBERRY SHORTCAKE

In the 1950s, Boston's renowned Durgin Park restaurant used to serve its colossal strawberry shortcake servings with the promise that anyone who could finish two would get a third, free. Inflation has done away with that promise, but a bystander at Durgin Park during such an attempt avers—"He tried, valiantly, but after a dinner of that famous roast beef slab with fixin's, plus two of those shortcakes, he never had a chance on the third!"

1½	cups flour
½	teaspoon salt
2	teaspoons baking powder
1	tablespoon sugar
6	tablespoons butter
½	cup milk
	Melted butter
2	quarts fresh strawberries, hulled and halved
1	cup sugar
1	cup whipped cream

Sift together flour, salt, baking powder, and sugar. Cut in butter until mixture is crumbly. With fork quickly stir in milk. Turn out onto floured board, divide into 2 pieces, and roll each piece out into rectangle ¼ inch thick. Brush 1 piece with melted butter, cover with second piece, and bake in 425°F. oven for 15–20 minutes. Separate layers and cool. Mix strawberries with sugar and let stand in bowl while shortcake cools. Then put a layer of shortcake on serving plate and spread with generous layer of sweetened strawberries. Repeat with second shortcake layer and top second strawberry layer with whipped cream. Serve immediately.

Serves 6.

SNOW CAKE

¼ cup butter
1 cup sugar
1½ cups cake flour
½ teaspoon salt
1 teaspoon baking powder
1 cup light, new-fallen snow (just scoop up a cupful—do not pack)
¼ cup milk
1 teaspoon vanilla
4 egg whites

The baking powder is simply a safeguard, as the leavening power (ammonia content) of new-fallen snow can vary considerably.

Cream together butter and ½ cup sugar. Sift together flour, salt, and baking powder, and blend into creamed mixture. Combine snow and milk, stir to form a mush, and add to flour mixture. Stir in vanilla. Beat egg whites until stiff and beat in remaining ½ cup sugar. Fold into batter. Bake in 2 greased 9-inch round cake pans at 350°F. for 35–45 minutes. Frost with Snow Icing (see below).

Makes 1 layer cake.

Snow Icing

1½ cups sugar
1½ teaspoons light corn syrup
½ cup boiling water
2 egg whites, beaten stiff
1 teaspoon vanilla

Combine sugar, corn syrup, and boiling water; bring to boil, and stir until sugar is dissolved. Continue boiling to soft-ball stage (when a drop of syrup in a cup of cold water forms a soft ball). Pour syrup over stiffly beaten egg whites, beating constantly. Add vanilla and continue beating 10–15 minutes until mixture reaches spreading consistency. (Place mixture over bowl of hot water if beating becomes difficult.)

Grandma's Christmas Album

by Jane Goyer

Every year, about mid-November, Grandma's Christmas Album was brought out from its hiding place so that Grandma might plan our Christmas. The cover was of bright red, soft leather-like material. At each corner, angels were pasted, white ones, with golden wings; and in the center, in golden script, the words—

CHRISTMAS ALBUM
All things bright and beautiful
All creatures great and small
All things wise and wonderful
The good Lord made them all.

The pages were shabby and worn, but contained some of the most delectable dishes ever tasted. On Christmas Eve, if there was any snow on the ground, we were pretty sure to have Snow Cake with Snow Icing. The cake really calls for a whole cupful of "newly fallen snow." [Ed. note: the ammonia content of fluffy, new-fallen snow acts as a leavening agent; as in Snow Griddle Cakes (see p. 125).]

If there were no snow on the ground, the choice might be Salt Pork Cakes, made from fat salt pork chopped fine and rich with molasses and spices [see p. 154]. There was also a "rule" for Election Cake [see p. 152], and one for Donation Cake, the latter often made to bring to funerals and sometimes called Funeral Cake! It contained chopped prunes and nut meats.

—Excerpt from December 1973 *Yankee*

Cookies

Cookies were an integral part of the homely perfume of the traditional Yankee kitchen; somehow the fragrance of just-baked cookies lingered on long after the cookies themselves had been stored in the stoneware crock in the pantry. These crocks, used also for pickles, dry ingredients, mincemeat, and a host of other useful purposes, still are one of the best means of storing cookies, and still can be purchased in New England farm stores. The tops are sold separately, so be sure you remember to purchase one that fits your crock.

Tea and Me

by Martha McChesney Wilkinson

"Now that you are in your teens, my dear, I think it is high time you started learning something about the art of being a hostess," said my stepmother soon after my thirteenth birthday. It seemed like rather a silly idea to me, but I had discovered it was a wise plan to go along with her suggestions, since she was a person of great determination.

"I think the first lesson will be the giving of a tea party," she continued briskly. "Choose five of your friends and invite them to come here at four o'clock next Thursday afternoon. In the meantime we will have a little lesson with the tea tray and I will show you just what you must do. It is important to learn the amenities early so when you are grown up you will never have to give a thought to them. They will be second nature!"

So out came the tea tray with the lovely Kirk silver service, the dainty Staffordshire cups and plates with the tiny pink rosebuds I so greatly admired, and the lesson began.

> *"Unless the teakettle boiling be*
> *Filling teapot spoils the tea,"*

quoted my stepmother gaily. Then she explained that the tea must be in the pot to steep for about five minutes before I offered it to my guests. "Give them a choice of milk or lemon, dear, and always pour in the milk before the tea, adding a little hot water if it appears too strong. Using these tongs, place a lump of sugar in the cup and another on the saucer. After that it is time to hand the guest the cup and saucer and one of these tea plates, also a serviette. When your guests have their tea Frank [our butler] will pass the buttered bread—it must be paper thin— the watercress sandwiches, and a little later the tea cakes and petits fours. I will instruct Violet (our cook) to make your favorite cookies for the occasion.

"When your guests have almost but not quite finished their tea," she continued, "ask if you may fill their cups. Never say, 'Will you have some *more* tea,' since that makes them appear greedy. Just say 'some tea.'"

We next took up the use of the soup bowl where cold tea was to be disposed of before pouring the fresh cup. We also discussed conversation. "It should be general," my stepmother said, "and everyone must be included. Here is a nice little rhyme you could mention. It is very appropriate:

> *A good cup of tea*
> *Is reported to be*
> *A famous restorer in sadness.*
> *It quickens the brain,*
> *Enlivens the frame,*
> *Infusing a spirit of gladness."*

I personally thought an orangeade or some soda pop would do more for me, but I didn't dare say so. I wondered vaguely if my guests wouldn't feel the same way? The next decision was the dress I should wear, and for once we were in complete agreement. "I will leave the selection of the guests entirely to you, Martha. This is your party," she concluded.

The week wore on and finally Thursday arrived. The chairs were arranged in a nice circle facing the tea table and fresh flowers were placed at strategic spots in the drawing room. When everything she could do ahead had been done, my stepmother put on her hat and said carefully, "I have decided that it would be better for me not to be here—it might make you self-conscious. So I am going out while the tea party is going on."

With a quiver of anticipation and some trepidation I seated myself behind the tea table and there I sat in solitary splendor. Frank peered around the door awaiting the signal to bring in the tray. I was pleased that I felt I really knew what to do and when to do it.

Then, all of a sudden, I had a dreadful sickening realization. In my preoccupation with preparing myself for the occasion I had completely forgotten to invite a single guest! It was a ghastly moment. I felt like crying, but on the other hand it struck me as quite funny, too. What would my stepmother say? Plenty no doubt. "It is going to be pretty bad," I thought. "Oh, well, I had better be fortified for what is coming," so I signalled old Frank to bring in the tray. I took a deep breath and poured a cup of tea while he looked on much mystified. I was careful to follow instructions to the letter and after taking a few sips I said brightly, "Have some tea, Martha," and I poured some more. With great relish I devoured practically all the bread and butter, the watercress sandwiches, the tea cakes, and the petits fours. The empty chairs before me didn't bother me much. I felt relieved that I didn't have to mention those ridiculous rhymes and for once I could be as greedy as I liked. I made the most of it, and I can't remember ever enjoying a tea party more.

—Excerpt from April 1976 *Yankee*

BUTTERMILK COOKIES

These taste even better the day after they are baked.

2　cups sugar
1　cup butter
1　cup buttermilk
1　teaspoon baking soda
3　eggs
¼　teaspoon nutmeg
½　teaspoon lemon juice
3　cups flour
　　Raisins

Cream sugar and butter. Beat in remaining ingredients to form smooth dough. Drop by teaspoons onto ungreased cookie sheet and bake in 350°F. oven for 10–12 minutes. Place a raisin in the center of each cookie while still hot.

Makes 6½ dozen.

DATE-FILLED COOKIES

Special enough to make as a holiday gift. Use kitchen shears to chop dates quickly and easily.

3　cups flour
1½　teaspoons baking powder
½　teaspoon salt
⅔　cup butter
½　cup brown sugar
1　egg, beaten
1　teaspoon vanilla
⅓　cup milk

Sift together flour, baking powder, and salt. Cream butter and sugar until light. Blend in egg and vanilla, and gradually beat in flour and milk until mixture is smooth. Chill dough thoroughly. Roll dough out to ⅛-inch thickness and cut out with 2½-inch round cookie cutter or rim of a juice glass. Place 1 teaspoon Date Filling (see below) on circle of dough; place a second circle of dough over filling and press edges together. Prick with fork. Bake on ungreased cookie sheet at 400°F. for 10–12 minutes.

Makes 3 dozen.

Date Filling

2　cups stoned, chopped
　　dates (or prunes)
½　cup sugar
⅔　cup hot water
1　tablespoon lemon juice
1　tablespoon butter

Combine dates, sugar, and hot water in saucepan and simmer 10 minutes, stirring frequently. Remove from heat, and add lemon juice and butter. Cool thoroughly before using to fill cookies.

COCONUT MACAROONS

Chewy cookies that are popular in several of Boston's oldest restaurants. Don't try to remove hot cookies from foil; the centers will stick.

3	egg whites
1½	cups confectioners' sugar
4	ounces grated coconut
½	teaspoon vanilla

Beat egg whites until stiff. Gradually work in confectioners' sugar, coconut, and vanilla to form a stiff paste. (Add a few drops of cream if mixture is too stiff.) Drop by teaspoons onto baking sheet lined with waxed paper or foil. Bake at 300°F. for 15–20 minutes or until light brown. Remove paper or foil from pans. Cool. Then remove macaroons to cake rack and let stand until cold.

Makes 3 dozen.

GINGERSNAPS

An old-time favorite that keeps for weeks in a covered jar.

1	cup butter
2	cups molasses
2	eggs
4	cups flour
2	teaspoons baking soda
½	teaspoon salt
2	tablespoons ginger

Cream butter with molasses. Beat in eggs. Sift together flour, soda, salt, and ginger, and add to egg mixture. Chill well. Roll out to ¼-inch thickness on lightly floured board, and cut with 2-inch cookie cutter or the rim of a juice glass. Place on greased cookie sheet and bake in 350°F. oven for 10 minutes.

Makes 4 dozen.

VERMONT MAPLE COOKIES

¾ cup butter
½ cup firmly packed brown
    sugar
1 egg
1 teaspoon vanilla
2¼ cups flour
2 teaspoons baking powder
½ teaspoon baking soda
½ teaspoon salt
½ cup maple syrup
½ cup chopped walnuts
    Walnut halves

Bring these on country hikes or picnics. Crisp and delicious.

Cream butter and sugar. Beat in egg and vanilla. Sift together flour, baking powder, soda, and salt, and add to creamed mixture alternately with maple syrup. Blend well and fold in nuts. Drop dough by rounded teaspoonfuls onto ungreased cookie sheet. Top each cookie with a walnut half. Bake 8–10 minutes at 400°F.

Makes 3 dozen.

LEMON SLICES

2 cups flour
1 cup butter
½ cup confectioners' sugar
4 eggs
2 cups sugar
½ teaspoon salt
6 tablespoons lemon juice
1 lemon rind, grated
4 tablespoons flour
2 teaspoons confectioners'
    sugar
    Confectioners' sugar

Attractive, crispy cookies that taste like lemon pie.

Mix together 2 cups flour, butter, and ½ cup confectioners' sugar. Press into greased 9-x-13-inch baking pan and bake at 350°F. for 25 minutes, or until lightly browned. As batter bakes, beat together eggs, sugar, salt, lemon juice, and rind. Sift together 4 tablespoons flour and 2 teaspoons confectioners' sugar and fold into egg mixture. Pour over baked crust and bake 35–40 minutes longer. Remove from oven and dust with confectioners' sugar. When cooled, slice into 1-x-2-inch bars.

Makes 5 dozen bars.

SUGAR COOKIES

½ cup butter
1 cup sugar
2 eggs
3 cups flour
½ teaspoon salt
2 teaspoons baking powder
½ cup milk
1 teaspoon vanilla

A perfect sugar cookie for Christmas or any other time of year.

Cream butter and sugar. Beat in eggs. Sift together flour, salt, and baking powder, and add to creamed mixture alternately with milk and vanilla. Chill dough well. On lightly floured board roll out chilled dough ⅛ inch thick and cut with cookie cutters. Bake on greased baking sheet in 375°F. oven for 10 minutes.

Makes 3–4 dozen.

9

PIES AND DESSERTS

Pies

No pie is worth its name without a tender, flaky pie crust to provide the proper environment for its filling. Here are some keys to success.

The secret to a tender crust lies in these basics: Don't touch the pastry with your hands; use ice-cold water; and bake two-crust pies in a preheated 450°F. oven for ten minutes, then turn heat down to 425°F. Check after another ten minutes—usually it is better at this time to reduce the oven heat again, to 350°F., at which temperature you cook the pie for the rest of the time specified in the recipe.

All this prevents the shortening from melting slowly and getting oily before it blends with the flour.

If, in a two-crust pie, edges brown too rapidly, take the pie from the oven, press a strip of aluminum foil over the edges of the pastry, and return to oven.

For a baked pie shell, the trickiest part is to fit the rolled-out pastry into the pie plate. This is easily done by rolling the pastry around the roller, transferring the roller to the top of the pan, unrolling the pastry over, and pressing it into, the pan. Prick the bottom a number of times; butter a square of aluminum foil large enough to be pressed into pie plate so that it covers both bottom and edges. Place foil, buttered side down, over pastry in pan. Bake at 450°F. for about ten minutes; when the shell is just beginning to be golden firm, remove foil lining, and bake for another three to five minutes.

Pies for Breakfast

by Barbara Radcliffe Rogers

A Yankee, to a European, is any American. To a Southerner, it's a Northerner; to a Northerner, it's a New Englander; to a New Englander, a resident of Maine, New Hampshire, or Vermont. But to those of us who are still not excluded by other definition, it's someone who eats pie for breakfast.

The breed is getting rarer, since most people don't eat anything for breakfast anymore—or not so's you'd notice. Pie for breakfast is a custom from the days when breakfast was a full and hearty meal eaten after a couple of hours of pre-dawn work had already taken place.

There was nothing instant about an old-fashioned farm breakfast. Women used to get up at 5:30 to bake hot biscuits every morning. Fresh doughnuts were not an unusual accompaniment to the day's first meal. But the breadstuffs were just that—they were not the main dish.

The breakfast menu wasn't complete without pie, even though the main course may have been ham or sausage or fried liver and onions. All kinds of berry and fruit pies were served in season, and dried or canned fruit was used when the fresh ran out. But everybody's favorite was mincemeat.

If hearty pies are too heavy for today's lighter, later breakfasts, a delectable wedge of homemade apple pie and a piece of store cheese will begin your day with more food value than a bowl of most commercial cold cereals. And it will certainly lift your spirits to greet the new day.

—Excerpt from article originally titled
"Eating Pies for Breakfast," in March 1978 *Yankee*

PLAIN PASTRY

An all-purpose pie crust.

2 **cups flour**
1 **teaspoon salt**
⅓ **cup lard**
⅓ **cup butter**
5 **tablespoons cold water**

Sift flour with salt. Cut in lard with pastry blender until it resembles cornmeal. Cut in butter until mixture resembles peas. Blend in water with a fork. Add more water if needed to make dough hold together in a ball. Divide dough into 2 parts, one slightly larger than the other. Roll each out on floured board, using larger part for bottom crust, smaller part for top crust.

Makes enough for one 2-crust 9-inch pie.

PASTRY FOR DOUBLE-CRUST 10-INCH PIE

For larger pies—9½ inches to 10 inches in diameter.

Mix flour with salt. Cut in shortening until mixture resembles fine meal. Add cold water until mixture "cleans the bowl." Chill for 30 minutes. Then roll out as directed in recipe for Plain Pastry (opposite page).

Makes enough for one 9½–10-inch 2-crust pie.

2⅔ cups flour
1 teaspoon salt
1 cup shortening
7 to 8 tablespoons cold water

RICH TART DOUGH

Richer and sweeter than plain pie crust. Good for open fruit pies.

Mix flour, salt, sugar, and butter with pastry blender. Beat egg yolk into 6 tablespoons water. Add to flour mixture. Pat together to form a ball, adding water if necessary. Roll out ¼ inch thick.

Makes enough for one 9-inch crust and lattice top, or for 6–8 tarts.

1½ cups flour
¾ teaspoon salt
1½ tablespoons sugar
8 tablespoons butter
1 egg yolk
6 to 8 tablespoons water

ALMOND SPONGE PIE

A rather luxurious, nutty custard pie.

Cream butter with lemon juice and rind. Add sugar gradually, creaming until fluffy. Beat egg yolks until light and add to sugar and butter mixture. Add almonds. Mix well. Beat egg whites with salt until stiff but not dry. Fold into mixture, blending lightly and thoroughly. Pour into pie shell. Bake in 350°F. oven for about 30 minutes or until a knife inserted in center of pie comes out clean. Cool.

Makes one 8-inch pie.

1 8-inch baked pie shell
2 tablespoons butter
2 teaspoons lemon juice
1 teaspoon grated lemon rind
¾ cup sugar
3 eggs, separated
½ cup chopped toasted almonds
½ teaspoon salt

BOILED CIDER PIE

1 8- or 9-inch unbaked pie
   shell
½ cup boiled cider
1 tablespoon butter
1 cup maple sugar
¼ cup water
⅛ teaspoon salt
¼ teaspoon nutmeg
¼ teaspoon cinnamon
2 eggs, separated

Boiled cider is a kind of "apple molasses," made by boiling down fresh cider (without added preservatives) to reduce it to one-third or one-quarter of its original measure.

Combine boiled cider, butter, maple sugar, water, salt, nutmeg, and cinnamon. Simmer 5 minutes until well blended. Cool. Beat egg yolks until light and lemon-colored and add to cooled cider mixture. Beat whites until stiff. Fold into cider mixture. Turn into pie shell. Bake in 350°F. oven for about 40 minutes, or until set.

Makes one 8- or 9-inch pie.

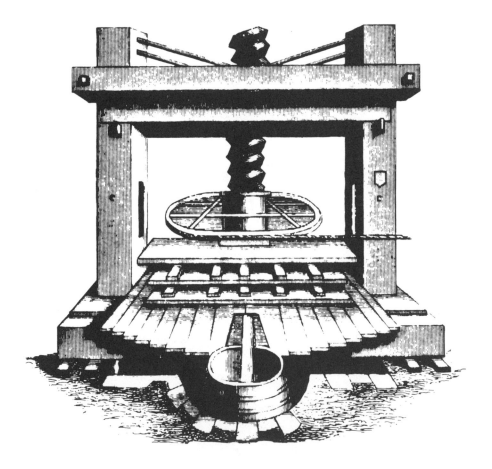

About Cider (and Boiled Cider)

by Arthur H. Parker

I can't remember just when my father began to operate his cider-mill but, from old accounts which I have been looking over, I know that it was some time prior to 1888. I began to participate, actively, in the activities of the mill early in the nineties, and from then on to the day when the last apple went through the press, I spent every free moment, busily and happily, with my father at the mill.

In its heyday our cider, boiled cider, and vinegar business was prosperous indeed. Among our customers we numbered not only the thirsty citizen with his one or two gallon earthenware jugs, but also big concerns like the Cunard Steamship Line and the Holbrook Grocery Co. One of our most interesting, and at the same time peculiar customers, was an individual who dealt in boiled cider and boiled cider applesauce. Regardless of the sugar content of the cider from which his product was made, each order was accompanied by the laconic stipulation—"six to one is what I want." This meant that six gallons of cider should be boiled down to one of the finished product. Sometimes he received a barrel of syrup and, not infrequently, a barrel of jam. But he was perfectly satisfied. "Six to one" was what he wanted and what he invariably received.

It seems hard to believe, in this day of so many scarcities, that the old timers did things in such a big way, particularly their cider business. Reading over the old ledger, containing the names of a majority of the farmers of our own and near-by towns, I see that one of our neighbors brought in 126 bushels of apples from which he took away 400 gallons of cider (about 8 casks) and for the making of which he paid just $6.39. Think of it. A gallon of delicious cider for a cent and a half and the labor of picking up the apples. Another neighbor brought in 130 bushels— took away 422 gallons—and paid eventually, I hope, $6.59.

—Excerpt from article originally titled
"The First Atom Bomb," in January 1947 *Yankee*

COFFEE ANGEL PIE

Do you suppose angel pies are so called because they are heavenly? This one has a marvelous café à la crème filling and is served frozen. A show-stopper.

Meringue Shell

4 egg whites
¼ teaspoon salt
¼ teaspoon cream of tartar
1 cup sugar
½ teaspoon vanilla

Beat egg whites with salt and cream of tartar until stiff. Then add sugar, a spoonful at a time, beating well after each addition. Beat in vanilla and pile in well-buttered 9- or 10-inch pie plate. With spatula, make meringue high around the sides and flat inside, to form a shell to hold filling. Bake for 1 hour at 275°F. or until meringue is just firm, but still white. Cool on cake rack while you make filling (see below).

Filling

1 can (14 ounces)
   sweetened
   condensed milk
1 cup strong black coffee,
   chilled
1½ cups whipping cream
1 cup finely chopped
   walnuts

Mix condensed milk with coffee until well blended. Whip cream until stiff. Fold cream into coffee mixture, blending well. Pour filling into meringue shell. Sprinkle generously with nuts. Freeze.

Makes one 9- or 10-inch pie.

LEMON CHIFFON PIE

1 9-inch baked pastry shell
   or cookie crust
3 tablespoons lemon gelatin
¼ cup boiling water
4 eggs, separated
¼ cup sugar
½ cup fresh lemon juice
¼ cup fresh orange juice
   Grated rind of 1 lemon
¼ cup sugar
1 cup heavy cream

From the melt-in-your-mouth department.

Dissolve gelatin in boiling water. Set aside. Beat egg yolks. Add ¼ cup sugar, then lemon and orange juice. Cook in double boiler over boiling water until thickened, stirring as needed. Add gelatin mixture and grated lemon rind. Cool to room temperature or cooler. Beat egg whites until stiff. Beat in remaining ¼ cup sugar. Fold into yolk mixture until well mixed. Place in pie shell. Refrigerate 2–3 hours until set. Whip cream and spread over pie just before serving.

Makes one 9-inch pie.

PAPER BAG APPLE PIE

Not an "upper crust" dessert, with its deliciously crunchy topping, this is a really fancy pie ridiculously easy to make.

1   **9-inch unbaked pie shell**
1   **cup sugar**
½   **cup plus 2 tablespoons flour**
1   **teaspoon cinnamon**
4   **to 5 large cooking apples, peeled, cored, and thinly sliced**
2   **teaspoons lemon juice**
½   **cup butter**

Preheat oven to 450°F. Combine ½ cup sugar, 2 tablespoons flour, and ½ teaspoon cinnamon. Sprinkle over apples and mix gently. Spoon into unbaked pie shell. Drizzle with 2 teaspoons lemon juice. Now combine ½ cup sugar, ½ cup flour, and ½ teaspoon cinnamon. Cut in butter until mixture is like fine meal. Pat this over top of pie. Slip pie into paper bag the right size to fit neatly over pie plate. Slide onto middle rack of oven. Tuck end of bag underneath plate. Bake 1 hour or until the bag just starts to scorch. Near the end of baking period you may slit bag with sharp knife and fold back for extra browning. The topping will be crisp and bubbly and—best of all—the bag will have caught any drippings. No smoke and no messy oven to clean!

Makes one 9-inch pie.

Mince Pie

by Beatrice H. Comas

Call it "Grete Pie," "Bakemete," "bakemete in coffyns," "mete custard," or "minc'd pye," mince pie has rather remarkably retained its popularity since it was invented, long before English cookbooks were written.

If you think there is a lot of peeling and chopping necessary to make "from scratch" mincemeat, consider the ingredients required for such a pie made in 1394: a pheasant, a hare, a capon, two partridges, two pigeons, two rabbits with their meat separated from the bones and chopped fine in a hash, livers and hearts of all these animals, two kidneys of sheep, little meat balls of beef with eggs, pickled mushrooms, salt, pepper, vinegar, and various spices. This was poured into the broth in which the bones had been cooked and "put all in a crust of good pastry and baked."

There is an old English saying, "The devil dares not show his face in Cornwall at Christmas lest he be baked in a pie."

We don't bake "four and twenty blackbirds" in our mince pies anymore, but Henry VIII and his daughter Elizabeth, who was more likely to grant a favor after being plied with sweets, might be just as pleased with the following mincemeat recipe, *and* surprised that "minc'd mete" is not just for "grete pyes" nowadays.

—Excerpt from article originally titled
"A Way with Mincemeat," in November 1979 *Yankee*

STRAWBERRY RHUBARB PIE

Pastry for 10-inch,
double-crust pie
(see p. 169)
2 cups sugar
½ cup flour
3 cups chopped rhubarb
3 cups hulled, halved
  strawberries
2 tablespoons butter, cut up

A combination invented to take advantage of the brief period in the spring when these two fruits can be had together, ripe; the marriage of flavors is a "natural." This recipe is designed for fresh fruit.

Line 10-inch pie pan with pastry. Combine sugar and flour and mix with rhubarb and strawberries. Pour into pie pan. Dot with butter. Cover with top crust. Make 2 slits in crust. Bake 10 minutes at 425°F., lower heat to 400°F. for 10 minutes, then bake at 375°F. until done, about 30 more minutes.

Makes one 10-inch pie.

MINCEMEAT

To an old-time Yankee, apple and mince were the pies. House-wives made mincemeat by the gallon and used it the same way. To make mince pie, simply fill an unbaked pie shell with mincemeat, cover with top crust and bake at 450° F. for about 30 minutes.

Mix together all ingredients except brandy in 10-quart kettle. Simmer 2 hours, stirring frequently. Cool. Add brandy. Mix thoroughly. Store in crock or jars in a cool place. Age for at least 2 weeks before using.

Makes about 8 quarts.

- 4 **pounds apples, peeled, cored, and sliced**
- 2 **pounds lean beef, chopped**
- 1 **pound beef suet, chopped**
- 3 **cups cider**
- 4 **cups brown sugar**
- 3 **pounds seeded raisins**
- 1½ **pounds currants**
- ½ **pound chopped citron**
- ¼ **pound candied orange peel**
- ¼ **pound candied lemon peel**
- **Juice and chopped rind of 1 orange**
- **Juice and chopped rind of 1 lemon**
- 2 **teaspoons nutmeg**
- 1 **tablespoon cinnamon**
- 1 **tablespoon allspice**
- 1 **teaspoon cloves**
- 1 **teaspoon salt**
- 1 **cup brandy**

YANKEE RASPBERRY TART

The crust is a little fussy, but the end result is well worth it.

Put flour on pastry cloth or board. Make a well in the center. Into it put the 3 hard-boiled egg yolks, sieved, the 4 raw egg yolks, shortening, sugar, coffee, lemon rind, and spices. Work center ingredients into a paste, then quickly work in flour. Roll out. Don't worry if it doesn't roll out easily. Just take the rolled pieces of dough and, pressing with your fingers, use them to line a shallow 9-inch pie plate. Make sure the dough layer is not too thin. Trim edges and save trimmings to make lattice top. Sprinkle bottom with bread crumbs. Fill with jam. Make lattice strips for top with remaining pastry. Brush strips with egg white; dust tart lightly with confectioners' sugar. Bake in 375°F. oven for about 35 minutes. Cool. Chill in refrigerator. Serve plain or with whipped cream.

Makes one 9-inch pie.

- 1½ **cups flour**
- 3 **hard-boiled egg yolks**
- 4 **raw egg yolks**
- 7 **tablespoons shortening**
- 7 **tablespoons sugar**
- 2 **tablespoons instant coffee**
- **Grated rind of 1 lemon**
- 1 **teaspoon cinnamon**
- ½ **teaspoon nutmeg**
- ¼ **cup fresh white bread crumbs**
- 2 **cups raspberry jam**
- 1 **egg white, lightly beaten**
- **Confectioners' sugar**

PUMPKIN OR SQUASH CHIFFON PIE

1   **9-inch pie shell, baked**
1   **tablespoon unflavored gelatin**
¼   **cup cold water**
3   **eggs, separated**
6   **tablespoons sugar**
1¼   **cups pumpkin or squash (cooked and mashed, or canned)**
½   **cup milk**
     Pinch salt
½   **teaspoon ginger**
1   **teaspoon cinnamon**
½   **teaspoon nutmeg**
6   **tablespoons sugar**
½   **cup whipping cream**

Them as prefers squash will never agree with them as prefers pumpkin, but here's a recipe good for both.

Soften gelatin in cold water. Set aside. Beat egg yolks until thick and lemon-colored. Add 6 tablespoons sugar, pumpkin or squash, milk, salt, and spices. Cook until thick in top of double boiler over boiling water. Add gelatin mixture. Cool. Beat egg whites until stiff. Add second 6 tablespoons sugar to egg whites, then fold into cooled pie mixture. Pour into pie shell and chill. Whip cream. Top with whipped cream and serve.

Makes one 9-inch pie.

Desserts

FRUIT DESSERTS

**("Slumps," "Grunts," "Pandowdys,"
"Bettys," and "Buckles")**

Stumped by slumps, grunts, buckles, bettys, and pandowdys? You are not alone. Confusion surrounds their names and origins. Despite their inelegant names, they *are* elegant desserts, which date back to the very beginnings of colonial New England. Fresh and dried fruits were staples found in every cellar or larder. Cooked with sweeteners (often molasses or maple syrup rather than the then-costly white sugar), topped with crust or dough, and served with sweet cream from the family cow, they made an easily prepared dessert suitable to the hard-working, calorie-consuming, sweet-loving inhabitants of a cold and rigorous climate.

These delicious and fruit-full desserts are just as popular now as ever, even though it is awfully hard to tell nowadays what's what. You may think a betty is always made with bread crumbs and apples until you try Pineapple Betty (p. 181). A pandowdy got its name from the fact that a cook would "dowdy" the crust by cutting it into the apples with a sharp knife either while it was cooking or just before serving. Well, no recipe tells you to do *that* today; in fact a pandowdy isn't necessarily made with apples! Where did "slump," "grunt," and "buckle" come from? There are lots of theories, but few facts. Does the topping of a buckle always *buckle* or collapse? Perhaps a slump slumps (and the biscuits *do*, into the fruit), but what does a *grunt* do? One old-timer tells you that "grunt" refers to the sound of satisfaction emitted after eating one; his wife states that a grunt is the white flour dumpling that you steam on top of the fruit. His daughter will say a slump always is fruit topped with biscuit dough; her mother begs to differ, asserting that pie pastry makes a better slump. Culinary historians declare that grunts are always steamed and slumps are always baked. Some insist that slumps require apples, and grunts never anything but berries. Don't listen to them. The Brown Betty Rule of slumps and grunts is: *There Is No Rule!* All you need is fruit, sweetening, some kind of dough, a casserole dish, and a stove, and you can be as imaginative, as authentic, and as successful as your forebears.

"My, That's Delicious . . ."

by Janet Hayward Mullins

Most of the well known and best loved apple varieties came into existence quite by accident.

Everyone—if they know no other—knows the Delicious apple. The first Red Delicious sprouted in the 1890s in the orchard of Jesse Hiatt, a Quaker in Peru, Iowa. Because it was a wild seedling that sprang up by itself outside of the regular row of trees, Hiatt twice cut it down. It grew back the third time larger than before. Hiatt felt compassion for the tough little tree and is purported to have said, "If thee must live, thee may."

It was ten years before the sturdy little tree blossomed and bore one strawberry-colored apple streaked with dark red. Jesse tasted this strange new apple and told his wife: "Ma, this is the best apple in the whole world." He never changed his mind.

Hiatt sent his "best apple in the world" (which he called Hawkeye) to fairs, where it was ignored in favor of better known varieties. He took samples of his apple wherever he went. For his trouble he got mentioned in *The Winterset News* as batty and touting an apple that was no good. Eleven years went by with nobody paying any attention to Jesse Hiatt and his apple.

In 1893 Hiatt sent four Hawkeyes to a fruit show in Louisiana, Missouri, sponsored by Stark Nurseries. The show offered prizes for the best, most promising, highest quality, and heaviest producing fruits. At last Hiatt's Hawkeye was to receive the attention it merited—it won first prize.

Mr. C. M. Stark, president of Stark Nurseries, upon taking his first bite exclaimed, "My, that's delicious, and that's the name for it!"

But fate wasn't quite ready to yield the stage front and center to the Delicious apple. In the excitement of the show someone had misplaced the name and address of the sender.

Mr. Stark, eager to find the owner of the magnificent apple, repeated his apple show and fruit fair the following year in hopes that the Delicious would again be an entry. As the entries arrived each was carefully scrutinized for the mystery apple. Finally on the day of the fair a barrel arrived from Peru, Iowa, bearing the name Jesse Hiatt and containing the magnificent Delicious apple.

Stark quickly bought the propagating rights. He was so convinced that the Delicious was the pinnacle of the apple world that he spent $750,000 on its debut. Mr. Stark knew his apples. The Red Delicious is now the world's most popular variety and is grown on every continent.

—Excerpt from article originally titled "If It Weren't for a Broken Heart (in 1796), There'd Be No McIntosh Apple Today," in September 1977 *Yankee*

APPLE PANDOWDY

No New England cookbook is complete without at least one recipe for Apple Pandowdy. The only question is—which one? There's a whole slew of 'em—all amazingly good, all certified as "traditional," and all amazingly different. The main difference, mind, is in the starch used with the apples. You can line the baking dish with bread, or cover the apples with pie crust, or with baking powder biscuits. Of course, New England being as much New England as ever, the controversies only start with the starch question. Here, just to add to the arguments, is a fairly recent, but delicious, version of this old favorite. Serve warm, and pass heavy cream.

9	apples at least 2¼ inches in diameter, peeled, cored, and cut in wedges
1	cup hot water
½	cup molasses
¾	cup sugar
3	tablespoons butter
3	tablespoons cornstarch
½	teaspoon cinnamon
½	teaspoon salt
2	cups flour
4	teaspoons baking powder
½	teaspoon salt
⅓	cup shortening
⅔	cup milk

Arrange apples in buttered 9-x-13-inch baking dish. Add water and bake in 425°F. oven for about 10 minutes, until apples are barely soft, stirring occasionally. In a saucepan boil together molasses, sugar, butter, cornstarch, cinnamon, and ½ teaspoon salt until thoroughly blended. Pour mixture over apples and stir gently. Mix flour, baking powder, and second ½ teaspoon salt in bowl. Cut in shortening as for biscuits. Add milk and mix. Roll dough ¼ inch thick. Cut in twelve 2½-inch rounds. Place biscuits over apples. Bake at 425°F. for about 12 minutes until browned. *Serves 12.*

OLD-FASHIONED APPLE SLUMP

Louisa May Alcott named her house in Concord Apple Slump after this dessert. Actually, this is a "grunt" rather than a "slump," but perhaps Miss Alcott balked at living in a house called Apple Grunt!

4	cups apples, peeled, cored, and thinly sliced
⅔	cup brown sugar
⅔	cup white sugar
½	cup water
1	teaspoon cinnamon

Combine apples, sugars, water, and cinnamon in a deep covered frying pan 11 inches in diameter. Bring to boil. Cover and cook for about 10 minutes. Do not let apples get too soft. Drop Dumpling Dough (see below) by spoonfuls on apple mixture. Cover and cook for 12 minutes until dumplings are done. Remove dumplings to dessert dishes and spoon apples over them. Serve with cream. *Serves 8.*

Dumpling Dough

Mix all ingredients together to form dough.

1½	cups flour
¼	teaspoon salt
1½	teaspoons baking powder
½	cup milk

AROUND CAPE HORN BROWN BETTY

4 cups sliced apples
½ cup brown sugar
¼ teaspoon nutmeg
   Juice and rind of ½ lemon
2 cups fresh bread crumbs
4 tablespoons butter
½ cup water

This brown betty recipe traveled from Maine around Cape Horn to San Francisco in a clipper ship in 1849. Here are the original directions.

"About eight crisp apples. (Peel in long spirals, toss peelings over shoulder; observe initials of future husband.) Slice apples. Sprinkle with sugar, fresh grated nutmeg, fresh lemon juice, grated lemon rind. Alternate layers of buttered, home-made white bread, crumbled. Bake 1 hour, slow oven, covered casserole. Last 10 minutes uncovered. Brown. Serve hot, with pitcher rich cream."

Those who like a little more precision may prefer the modern version!

Place half of the apples in buttered 2-quart casserole dish. Mix brown sugar and nutmeg and sprinkle over apples, along with a little lemon juice and rind. Cover with bread crumbs and dot with butter. Repeat layers. Pour water over all. Cover dish and bake 1 hour at 350°F., removing the cover for last 10 minutes of cooking time to brown crumbs.

Serves 4.

BLACKBERRY GRUNT

FRUIT MIXTURE
1 quart blackberries
1 cup sugar
   (approximately)
½ cup water
2 tablespoons butter

CRUST
1 cup flour
1½ teaspoons baking powder
¼ teaspoon salt
2 tablespoons sugar
½ cup milk
2 tablespoons melted butter

Biscuits rather than dumplings top this; so perhaps it is really a "slump," though the taste certainly qualifies it for that "grunt" of satisfaction. Use with any berries, adjusting sugar to taste. Serve warm with cream.

Bring fruit mixture to a boil in a wide 2-quart saucepan with a lid. Mix together crust ingredients. Spoon over berries. Cover tightly. Simmer without lifting cover for 12 minutes. Biscuit is cooked when knife inserted in center comes out clean.

Serves 6.

BLUEBERRY BUCKLE

A popular Yankee dessert reminiscent of a cottage pudding, but with a separate sauce. If you have any cake left over you can serve it plain for breakfast. The sauce as given here is perfect for this dessert. For other purposes, where you might wish a thicker lemon sauce, beat an extra egg yolk in with the one egg specified in Lemon Sauce directions.

Cream sugar and butter. Add eggs. Mix thoroughly. Stir in milk. Sift together, then stir in flour, baking powder, salt, and nutmeg. Fold in blueberries. Spread in greased 8-inch-square pan. Combine topping ingredients. Mix until crumbly, then sprinkle over batter. Bake in 375°F. oven for 45 minutes until top springs back when lightly touched. Cut in squares and serve warm with Lemon Sauce (see below).

Makes sixteen 2-inch squares.

CAKE
¾ cup sugar
¼ cup butter
2 eggs, beaten
½ cup milk
1½ cups flour
2 teaspoons baking powder
½ teaspoon salt
1 teaspoon nutmeg
2 cups fresh or dry-pack frozen blueberries

TOPPING
½ cup sugar
½ cup flour
½ teaspoon cinnamon
¼ cup soft butter

Lemon Sauce

In 1-quart saucepan, cream butter and sugar. Add egg, lemon juice, rind, and ½ cup boiling water, beating well to blend all the ingredients. Stir over low heat for about 10 minutes until sauce thickens slightly. Do not boil.

Makes 2 cups.

½ cup butter
1 cup sugar
1 egg, well beaten
3 tablespoons lemon juice
1 tablespoon grated lemon rind
½ cup boiling water

PINEAPPLE BETTY

The cinnamon combines with the pineapple and graham crackers to create a marvelous "betty." Serve hot or cold with whipped cream or ice cream.

Combine sugar, lemon rind, and cinnamon. Put a layer of graham cracker pieces in bottom of greased 1-quart casserole dish; then add half the pineapple. Top with half the sugar mixture. Put in another layer of graham crackers, then remaining pineapple. Top with remaining graham cracker crumbs combined with remaining sugar mixture. Dot well with butter. Place in 400°F. oven and bake until top is brown and crusty.

Serves 4–6.

½ cup light brown sugar
1 teaspoon grated lemon rind
1½ teaspoons cinnamon
15 graham crackers, crumbled
3 cups diced canned pineapple
4 tablespoons butter

CHERRY PUDDING

This is closely related to cherry cobbler.

2   cups stewed dark red
    sweet cherries
⅓   cup butter
1   cup flour
¼   teaspoon soda
1   teaspoon cream of tartar
    (or 2 teaspoons baking
    powder)
    Pinch salt
¼   teaspoon nutmeg
1   cup milk

Drain cherries, reserving juice for sauce. Melt butter in 2-quart baking dish. Sift together dry ingredients, and slowly stir in milk.

Pour mixture into baking dish over melted butter. Spoon cherries into center. Bake at 375°F. for 40–50 minutes, or until a cake tester comes out clean. Let the pudding sit for 10 minutes to be sure it has set before serving with Cherry Pudding Sauce (see below).

Serves 6.

Cherry Pudding Sauce

Reserved cherry juice
1   cup water
2   tablespoons cornstarch
½   cup cold water
3   tablespoons sugar
1   tablespoon butter
    Whipped cream (optional)

Heat cherry juice with 1 cup water to boiling. Stir in cornstarch mixed with ½ cup cold water, sugar, and butter. Cook and stir until sauce thickens. Serve in sauce boat, with a bowl of whipped cream if desired.

RASPBERRY SLUMP

Now this is a "slump!" Try it with cherries or peaches as well, adjusting sugar to taste. Serve with cream or ice cream.

FRUIT MIXTURE
1   quart raspberries
1   cup sugar
½   cup water

CRUST
1   cup flour
2   teaspoons baking powder
⅛   teaspoon salt
4   tablespoons sugar
2   tablespoons butter
1   cup milk

Heat fruit, sugar, and water in buttered 2-quart baking dish in 400°F. oven. Mix flour with baking powder, salt, and sugar. Cut in butter until mixture resembles fine meal. Add milk, a little at a time, mixing after each addition. Spoon over hot berries. Bake at 400°F. for 20 minutes.

Serves 6.

PUDDINGS

Before the days of central heating, food performed an important warming function. Puddings which could be boiled or baked for a long time and kept warm on a wood stove were popular desserts. Made with variable amounts of milk, flour, cornmeal, molasses or maple syrup, suet, and apples or other dried fruit, they both warmed the body with much-needed calories and satisfied the sweet tooth. The advent of inexpensive oil or gas heat channeled tastes towards lighter and less caloric desserts, but now that oil and bottled gas are so expensive, who knows but what puddings may once again become popular! Most puddings here included are those that have survived the radical change (since they were invented) in house-heating, and are favorites today. They arc still nourishing and still heart-warming!

INDIAN PUDDING

Some Indian puddings are more like cereal than dessert. This light and delicious version is definitely dessert. Serve with cream or ice cream.

¼	cup molasses
3	tablespoons cornmeal
3½	cups milk, scalded
1	egg, beaten
½	cup sugar
½	teaspoon salt
½	teaspoon ginger
½	teaspoon cinnamon
2	tablespoons butter
½	cup cold milk

Add molasses and cornmeal to scalded milk. Stir to mix, and cook gently, stirring, until thick. Remove from heat. Blend egg, sugar, salt, ginger, and cinnamon. Add to cornmeal mixture. Pour into greased 1-quart casserole. Bake 30 minutes in 325°F. oven. Add butter and cold milk. Do not stir, but continue baking for about 1 hour.

Serves 4.

CHOCOLATE BREAD PUDDING

1   cup soft stale
    bread crumbs
2   squares unsweetened
    chocolate
1¼   cups sugar
1⅓   cups milk
2   tablespoons butter
2   eggs
¼   teaspoon salt
½   teaspoon vanilla
⅔   cup milk

The special consistency of a bread pudding combined with chocolate makes this a winner. Serve cold with whipped cream.

Cook crumbs, chocolate, sugar, and 1⅓ cups milk in double boiler until smooth. Add butter. Remove from heat. Beat eggs until light, and add salt, vanilla, and ⅔ cup milk. Add to chocolate mixture. Cook over hot water until thick. Pour into buttered 1½-quart baking dish. Bake at 350°F. for 20 minutes.

Serves 4.

PLUM PUDDING

½   pound raisins, chopped
½   pound golden raisins
¼   pound candied peels
¼   pound chopped figs
½   pound finely chopped
    beef suet
4   cups finely diced
    fresh bread crumbs
½   cup flour
½   teaspoon salt
½   teaspoon cinnamon
¼   teaspoon cloves
½   cup brown sugar
1   cup brandy
6   eggs, beaten
¼   cup brandy

While you're at it, make two and give one to a friend. The only trouble is, she'll want another one next year.

Mix fruits together. Add suet, crumbs, and flour to which salt and spices have been added. Next add sugar, 1 cup brandy, and eggs. Mix well. Fill two 1½-quart molds each about ⅔ full, and tie oiled paper over mold tops. Place molds in large pot on top of stove. Add enough boiling water to come ¾ up sides of molds. Cover pot and steam for 6 hours, adding water if necessary to maintain the level. Unmold. Warm another ¼ cup brandy, ignite, and pour over pudding just before serving. Serve with Pudding Sauce (see below). *Or,* cool and refrigerate for at least 3 weeks. (Pudding will keep in refrigerator or freezer up to a year.) To reheat for serving, steam as above for 2 hours.

Makes two 1-quart puddings.

Pudding Sauce

2   egg yolks
1   cup confectioners' sugar
½   teaspoon vanilla
⅛   teaspoon nutmeg
½   cup whipping cream

Beat egg yolks, add sugar, vanilla, and nutmeg, and beat until smooth. Whip cream, and fold into mixture.

Makes 1½ cups.

Favorite New England Recipes

Imogene Wolcott, author of the excellent and now sadly out of print *Yankee Cookbook* (Coward-McCann, 1939), compiled her book from the files of *Yankee* magazine, for which she was Food Editor for a number of years, and from recipes contributed to her as a result of her daily radio program over the "Yankee Network" for First National Stores. Interviewed in Boston in connection with her then-forthcoming *Yankee Cookbook* ("the finest plain cooking in the world"), the author offered her own selection of the 20 most typical New England recipes, basing her selections on the number of recipes sent in as a result of her daily broadcast. The three hundred and seventy-some versions of Indian pudding contributed headed the list in number, as reflected in the following list. Indian Pudding, by the way, was so called not because it came from the Indians, as corn did, but because it was made from Indian (corn) meal, rather than from the finer wheat flour to which the colonists had been accustomed in England. Here's Mrs. Wolcott's list—

1. Indian pudding
2. Boston baked beans
3. Boston brown bread
4. Parker House rolls
5. Clam chowder
6. Johnnycake
7. Codfish balls
8. Yankee pot roast
9. New England salt fish dinner
10. Split-pea soup
11. Red flannel hash
12. Fish chowder
13. Apple pandowdy
14. Green tomato pickle
15. Vermont turkey
16. Cranberry sauce
17. Pumpkin pie
18. Coleslaw
19. Scalloped oysters
20. Broiled lobster

6   slices white bread
4   cups diced rhubarb
¾   cups each brown and
      white
        sugar, or 1 cup maple
        syrup, or 1 cup honey
½   teaspoon cinnamon
½   teaspoon nutmeg
1½ cups hot milk
4   eggs

RHUBARB PUDDING

A wonderful way to welcome in the rhubarb season. Serve warm with vanilla ice cream.

Layer 2 slices bread, half the rhubarb, and half the sweetening and spices in a 2-quart casserole. Repeat, ending with last 2 slices bread. Pour hot milk over all. Beat 4 eggs slightly and pour over top. Bake 1 hour in 350°F. oven.

Serves 8–10.

LIGHTER DESSERTS AND ICE CREAMS

The strong development of international trade in New England, as its clipper ships flew around the world, racing from port to port with exotic cargoes and all sails set, brought considerable refinement to the Yankee diet. The Whaling Fleet played an important role, too, helping the clippers to usher in an era of enormous prosperity. Like OPEC and Texas today, the whaling merchants held a virtual monopoly on oil—whale oil—which was sold to light lamps as far away as China. And the clippers brought rare and hitherto prohibitively expensive ingredients (rice, white sugar in loaves, vanilla, coffee, and spices like nutmeg, cloves, mace, and ginger) regularly into the region in profitable trade, so that they became generally available and accessible to more modest pocketbooks.

Custards, flavored creams, rice puddings, and, later, gelatin desserts and soufflés crept into the cuisine, used as light and elegant settings for native fruits. Also favoring the new, more delicate desserts was the progress from scattered, small farms to towns and cities, where residents lived and worked in efficiently heated buildings at more sedentary jobs requiring less, little, or none of the manual labor required on the farm.

The Industrial Revolution and the Age of Invention also had culinary implications. One invention particularly pertaining to this chapter was the invention of the ice cream freezer! In fact, ice cream itself is a particularly American, and particularly New England invention, one that any region could pardonably pride itself on.

APRICOT SOUFFLÉ

A light but impressive ending to a dinner at any time of year.

Melt butter and stir in flour. When blended, add milk. Cook, stirring, over medium heat until thickened, making certain mixture does not boil. Remove from heat. Add lemon juice and jam or cooked, sweetened pulp. Beat in egg yolks and sugar. Beat egg whites until stiff and fold in. Pour into 1½-quart soufflé dish, buttered and dusted with sugar. Set in pan of hot water in 350°F. oven. Bake 35–40 minutes. Serve at once.

Serves 6.

2	tablespoons butter
3	tablespoons flour
¾	cup milk
2	teaspoons lemon juice
½	cup apricot jam or cooked, sweetened apricot pulp
4	eggs, separated
4	tablespoons sugar

BOSTON CHOCOLATE SPONGE

A delight for the chocolate addict.

Dissolve gelatin in water. Put chocolate in double boiler over simmering water. Add butter and milk. Stir until melted. Remove from heat. Add well-beaten egg yolks, stirring until well mixed. Cook slowly for about 1 minute. Remove from heat. Add gelatin mixture. Fold in stiffly beaten egg whites. Pour into 1½-quart mold that has been rinsed in cold water. Chill until firm. Turn out. Serve with whipped cream.

Serves 8.

1	tablespoon unflavored gelatin
¼	cup warm water
½	pound dark sweet chocolate
2	tablespoons butter
½	cup evaporated milk
4	eggs, separated
1	cup whipped cream

QUEEN OF PUDDINGS

A royal custard base, robed in jam and crowned with a majestic meringue. For a lighter touch, try substituting for the raspberry jam an equal amount of your favorite jelly or jam whipped with a fork to spreading consistency.

Beat egg yolks until thick and lemon-colored. Beat in ⅓ cup sugar, milk, cream, and grated lemon rind. Stir in bread crumbs. Pour into 2-quart casserole dish. Bake at 350°F. for 40–45 minutes until custard is set and top starts to brown. Spread with jam. Dust with nutmeg. Beat egg whites until stiff; slowly beat in ½ cup sugar. Spread meringue on top of jam. Bake at 450°F. for 5 minutes, or until meringue is lightly browned. Serve cold.

Serves 6–8.

4	eggs, separated
⅓	cup sugar
3	cups milk
1	cup light cream
	Grated rind of 1 lemon
2	cups fresh white bread crumbs
¾	cup raspberry jam
	Dusting nutmeg
½	cup sugar

LEMON SPONGE CUPS

An easy recipe that actually wants to be made a day ahead to allow the flavor to mellow.

1 tablespoon butter
1 cup sugar
4 tablespoons flour
　Pinch salt
5 tablespoons lemon juice
　Grated rind of 1 lemon
3 eggs, separated
1½ cups milk

Cream butter and sugar; add flour, salt, lemon juice, and lemon rind. Stir in egg yolks beaten with milk; fold in stiffly beaten egg whites. Turn into 8 greased custard cups or greased 1½-quart casserole dish, and set in pan containing enough hot water to come half-way up cups. Bake at 350°F. for 45 minutes. Cool. The custard will be at the bottom while the sponge cake will stay on top.

Serves 8.

CIDER SHERBET

A refreshing and novel summer ice, citrus-flavored. To freeze in two refrigerator trays, halve this recipe.

4 cups fresh cider
½ cup sugar
1 cup fresh-squeezed
　　orange juice
　Juice of 2 lemons

Simmer cider and sugar together for 5 minutes. Cool. Add juices. Freeze in hand freezer, using equal parts salt and ice. Eat right away.

Serves 12.

MOTHER'S APRICOT ICE CREAM

If you have an ice cream freezer and a taste for old-fashioned sherbet-like ice cream, this is for you. Note that the amounts given in this recipe are for a one-gallon *freezer.*

⅔ quart canned apricots,
　　drained
1 package (3 ounces) lemon
　　gelatin
1 cup hot water
2 cups sugar
½ cup plus 1 tablespoon
　　lemon juice
1 pint cream
　Milk as needed

Puree apricots in sieve, food grinder, or blender. Dissolve gelatin in hot water. Add sugar, lemon juice, and cream. Blend into apricots. Pour mixture into 1-gallon freezer container, and add enough milk to fill container. Pack and freeze.

Serves 18–20.

INDEX